How to
Protect
and
Manage
Your

401(k)

HOW TO
PROTECT
AND
MANAGE
YOUR

401(k)

Elizabeth Opalka, CPA, Esq.

CAREER
PRESS

Franklin Lakes, NJ

HOW TO PROTECT AND MANAGE YOUR 401(K)
EDITED BY JODI BRANDON
TYPESET BY STACEY A. FARKAS
Cover design by DesignConcept
Printed in the U.S.A. by Book-mart Press

To order this title, please call toll-free 1-800-CAREER-1 (NJ and Canada: 201-848-0310) to order using VISA or MasterCard, or for further information on books from Career Press.

The Career Press, Inc., 3 Tice Road, PO Box 687,
Franklin Lakes, NJ 07417
www.careerpress.com

Library of Congress Cataloging-in-Publication Data

Opalka, Elizabeth.
    How to protect and manage your 401(k) / by Elizabeth Opalka.
       p. cm.
    Includes bibliographical references and index.
    ISBN 1-56414-660-X (pbk.)
       1. 401(k) plans—Management. 2. Portfolio management—United States.
    3. Retirement income—United States—Planning. I. Title.

HD7105.45.U6063 2003
332.024'01—dc21   2003043453

Acknowledgments

The author is grateful to the following individuals for their help and encouragement:

- Richard Pagel, for proofreading every stage of this project, from the query letter to the book proposal to the final manuscript.

- Alison Picard, literary agent, for finding a publisher for this book.

- Mike Lewis, Senior Acquisitions Editor of Career Press, for taking an interest in the proposal for this book.

- Stacey Farkas, Editorial Director of Career Press.

- Mary Lou Opalka, Ed Opalka, Michael Opalka, Teresa Bisnett, Mary Liz Pillsworth, and Linda Barnas, for their comments and suggestions.

- Selina Sutchu, my 11-year-old daughter, for her patience with her mother's choice of a "boring" topic.

Contents

Note to
the Reader

THIS BOOK INTRODUCES GENERAL CONCEPTS RELATED to managing an individual's 401(k) account. In providing this information to the public, the author and publisher are not rendering legal, tax, investment, or other professional advice. If a reader requires professional advice tailored to a particular situation, he or she should seek the services of an appropriate professional.

The opinions and interpretations expressed in this book belong to the author and do not necessarily reflect those of her employer or any other organization. The author welcomes readers' comments sent by e-mail to *ElizabethOpalka@aol.com.*

Introduction

THE 401(k) MILLIONAIRE DREAM HAS DIED—a victim of stock-market declines, over-investment in employer stock, and stories of employer misconduct. And if proposed legislation becomes law, all 401(k) accounts will be renamed Employer Retirement Savings Accounts (ERSAs). Your 401(k) account would automatically become an ERSA.

The basic idea would remain the same. With your ERSA, you would be able to defer a portion of your pay up to $12,000 in 2003 (increasing to $13,000 in 2004, $14,000 in 2005, and $15,000 in 2006). In addition, once you reach age 50, you would be able to make an additional catch-up contribution of $2,000 per year (increasing to $3,000 in 2004, $4,000 in 2005, and $5,000 in 2006). Your employer would be able to match your contributions. Distributions from your ERSA would be taxable as ordinary income.

However, ERSAs would replace not only 401(k) accounts, but also SIMPLE 401(k) accounts, 403(b) accounts, governmental 457 accounts, salary reduction simplified employee pensions (SARSEPs), and SIMPLE IRAs. ERSAs would not replace nongovernmental 457 accounts. SIMPLEs, SARSEPs, 403(b) plans, and governmental 457 plans would be able to continue to exist indefinitely, but they would not accept any contributions after 2004.

The proposed legislation would also create two new consolidated savings accounts: Lifetime Savings Accounts (LSAs) and Retirement Savings Accounts (RSAs). You would also be able to convert certain types of existing accounts into these new accounts in order to consolidate and simplify your savings.

President George W. Bush proposed this (and other sweeping changes in the pension law) on February 3, 2003. Under the proposed legislation, an LSA could be used for any type of saving purpose, including a child's education, a new home, medical expenses, or a new business. You would be allowed to contribute up to $7,500 per year to an LSA and make penalty-free withdrawals at any time—with no holding period. The annual $7,500 contribution limit would be indexed for inflation in future years.

As is the case with contributions to current-law Roth IRAs, LSA contributions would not be deductible but earnings would accumulate tax-free. LSA distributions would be tax free, as well.

Unlike a Coverdell Education Savings Account (ESA) or Archer Medical Savings Account (MSA), your LSA would not require you to carefully plan future qualified expenses and allocate your savings among different types of tax-preferred accounts. You would also not have to figure out complicated rules or document qualified expenses.

Under the proposal, you could convert balances in an MSA, ESA, or 529 plan account to a LSA before January 1, 2004. Converting an MSA would be taxable, but converting an ESA or 529 plan account would not. However, balances in these accounts would not be convertible to LSAs after 2003.

In contrast to LSAs, Retirement Savings Accounts (RSAs) would be used only for retirement saving. The new RSA is intended to improve and simplify your savings opportunities by consolidating traditional IRAs, nondeductible IRAs, and Roth IRAs into one streamlined type of account. The rules would be similar to current-law Roth IRAs.

Your existing Roth IRA would be renamed an RSA. You would be allowed to make the maximum $7,500 contribution even if your income exceeds current income limits.

You would be allowed to contribute up to $7,500 per year to an RSA—in addition to amounts that you contribute to an LSA. The $7,500 contribution limit will be indexed for inflation in future years. As with contributions to current-law Roth IRAs, contributions would not be deductible but earnings would accumulate tax-free. RSA distributions after age 58 (or death or disability) would be tax-free.

Your existing traditional and nondeductible IRAs would be convertible into RSAs. Such accounts that you don't convert to RSAs would not be able to accept any new contributions (other than rollover contributions). However, you wouldn't be required to convert.

You would be able to convert your traditional IRA to an RSA at any time, regardless of your income level. The amount that you convert to an RSA would generally be taxable. If you convert before January 1, 2004, you would be able to spread the conversion tax over four years. If you convert after 2003, the total amount of the conversion tax would be due in the year of the conversion.

The introduction of the LSA and the RSA would significantly increase your opportunities to earn tax-free returns on your savings. If you are married and you and your spouse contributed the maximum $7,500 contribution to each type of account, the two of you would be saving $30,000 per year.

You would be also able to contribute to an LSA on behalf of other family members even if they don't have wage income. Using the LSA would be an appropriate strategy for saving for college tuition.

You might be tempted to compare the merits of after-tax saving through the LSA and RSA versus pre-tax saving through your employer's ERSA. For more information about tax traps associated with pre-tax savings plans, see Chapter 3.

Even with all these proposed changes, the recent lessons of 401(k) investing are as relevant as ever. The new savings accounts won't make stock market volatility go away. They also can't eliminate the vulnerability that comes from heavy investment in employer stock.

The old financial worries about retirement haven't changed either: Will you have enough money to retire at your target retirement age?

If you live to a ripe old age, will you outlive your money? If you are already retired, will you be forced to make drastic changes in your lifestyle—maybe even return to work?

There's good reason to be concerned. Even before the recent stock market malaise, the typical American retiree was sinking into more financial insecurity. In 1989, almost 30 percent of retired Americans lived on less than half of their pre-retirement incomes, according to the Economic Policy Institute. By 1998, the percentage of financially stretched retirees grew to 42.5 percent.

Since 1999, American household net worth has decreased every year. This is a significant reversal of the previous trend of ever-growing American household wealth, which began at the end of World War II.

As one of the largest components of the average household balance sheet, retirement savings need a serious review. This book offers some advice about what you can do to protect your financial future.

Chapter 1

Protecting Your 401(k) from Market Volatility

"It requires a great deal of boldness and a great deal of caution to make a fortune, and when you have got it, it requires ten times as much wit to keep it."

—Ralph Waldo Emerson

WHAT'S THE BEST WAY TO AVOID the ups and downs of the stock market? For starters, consider the obvious: Keep your 401(k) investments out of the stock market.

While you're at it, stay out of bonds, too. If today's low interest rates rise, the value of bonds—and bond funds—will fall. Bond funds would also fall if enough bond issuers defaulted.

If your only goal is protection, put your money in the stable value investment choice (a money market fund or guaranteed investment contract) that your 401(k) plan offers. Of course, if you put 100 percent of your 401(k) money into a stable value investment, your annual returns will barely keep you ahead of inflation. That doesn't compensate you for having to wait years to spend your money.

What if there's a good chance that stocks and bonds will earn higher returns than stable value investments? Can you afford to take that chance? If you take that chance, but it doesn't pay off in the end, will you have to work in your old age to make ends meet—or maybe even do without the basics?

Suppose you think that you may be able to risk some of your money. The question now becomes this: How much can you afford to lose?

Generally speaking, the older you are, the less you can afford to lose. That's because older individuals have fewer, if any, years of paid work ahead of them to make up for losses in the securities markets. Younger individuals, on the other hand, have time to make up for any short-term losses.

Here's a rule of thumb that may help you decide how much of your 401(k) money you can afford to lose this year. Simply subtract your age from 100 percent. Multiply the result by the balance in your 401(k) account. That's how much you can afford to lose.

> **Example.** Suppose you are 40 years old. The balance in your 401(k) account is $50,000. Using the rule of thumb, this year you can afford to lose 60 percent of $50,000, which is $30,000.

How do feel about that? Okay? Or I can't afford to lose that?

Remember that feeling. Because the next part of the rule of thumb is this: Put the amount you can afford to lose into stocks or a stock fund. Or invest your money according to how you would feel about losing it.

Is this approach too radical? Consider the fact that, in the first three years of the new millennium, most stock funds lost value. Losses in 401(k) accounts may be what caused many individuals aged 55 to 64 to delay retirement or go back to work during this period, according to the U.S. Bureau of Labor Statistics. During the same time period, stable value investments outperformed almost all stock funds—and some bond funds.

Don't stocks go up in more years than they go down? Historically, yes. Since 1926, the average annual return of the Standard & Poors

500, a benchmark of the American stock market, has been 11 percent. For years stocks have been touted as the best long-term retirement investment. But there's no guarantee of what will happen in the future—short term or long term.

What causes stock market volatility?

No one knows for sure how investors, as a group, decide how much individual stocks are worth, but there are two main schools of thought. One school of thought is sometimes called behavioral finance. The other school of thought is usually called fundamental analysis.

Behavioral finance starts with the truism that a thing is worth what people are willing to pay for it. Then it asserts that people are predictable as to how much they will pay for the thing in the future. If an investor perceives that people will pay a higher price for the thing in the future, the investor buys the thing at today's lower price. Later the investor sells the thing—at a profit or a loss—to another investor who perceives a higher price for the thing in the future. And so on.

In contrast, fundamental analysis concentrates on the benefits of the thing itself. If the thing is a share of stock, then one of its benefits is the company's payment of a dividend to the stockholder. If a profitable company pays little or no dividends but wisely reinvests its earnings in company operations, that can also be a benefit to the stockholder. Because a company must have earnings in order to pay dividends or to reinvest in operations, earnings are said to determine the fundamental value of the stock. As the company's earnings increase, the price of the company's stock goes up.

According to behavioral finance, stock prices go up and down because investors change their perceptions of what people will be willing to pay for the stock in the future. According to fundamental analysis, stock prices go up and down as companies' expected earnings go up and down. Some individuals think that the two schools of thought are inconsistent. Other individuals see truth in both schools of thought.

Those who believe in behavioral finance say that extreme investor optimism causes stock market booms and extreme investor pessimism causes stock market crashes. The history of financial markets shows an apparent pattern of overly optimistic speculative buying followed by panic, which is followed by a crash of market prices, which is followed by a pessimistic withdrawal from the markets.

A speculative boom often begins when a major new development in technology raises investors' optimistic outlook. One speculative boom in the stock market occurred in the late 1920s. Another one occurred in the late 1990s.

The 1920s were marked by technological innovations in telephone, radio, and automobiles. The United States also enjoyed unsurpassed prosperity, which led to a heightened faith in American business. Optimism about the American stock market led to speculative buying.

In the late 1990s, the Internet similarly fueled Americans' imaginations. Investors saw great promise in a new industry of start-up dot-com companies. The telecommunications industry also looked golden.

There was a catch: Many of the new technology companies didn't have any earnings, yet. Nevertheless, investors saw great potential.

At some point in a stock market boom, a shock to the financial system convinces some individuals that stocks are overpriced. The shock could be the unexpected failure of a high-profile product, a major corporate bankruptcy, or the corruption of business or government leadership. When there are more pessimistic individuals who want to sell their stock than there are optimistic buyers, stock prices go down. And they stay down—until investors perceive another reason to be optimistic.

In the 1920s, American business was booming, whereas Europe suffered severe economic problems. Eventually, confidence in the American business outlook began to erode. The crash of 1929 followed.

Similarly, the effects of a 1998 international economic crisis were largely confined to Asia. Foreign capital, looking for safety, flooded the United States. Beginning in 2000, though, more American technology companies ran out of their start-up cash and closed their doors. Technology stock prices fell sharply beginning in April 2000.

In 2001, a record 257 American public companies filed for bankruptcy, and in December 2001, Enron Corporation, the seventh-largest American company in terms of sales, suddenly filed for bankruptcy, too. (See Appendix A for details.) WorldCom, the second-largest telecommunications company in the world, filed for bankruptcy in July 2002. Massive accounting fraud allegedly brought down both companies.

Investors worried. How many other Enrons and WorldComs were there? Nobody knew. Many investors assumed the worst. The markets plunged.

Behavioral finance says that investors are basically irrational. In contrast, fundamental analysis says that investors are rational. A rational investor buys stock in a company that has earnings because only a company with earnings can pay dividends.

According to fundamental analysis, nothing matters as much as corporate earnings. That's because there's a limit to what rational investors will pay for a certain level of earnings per share.

This price limit can be seen in a stock's price-earnings (P/E) ratio. The P/E ratio is the stock's current market price divided by its earnings per share.

> **Example.** The price of company A's stock is $100. The company's annual earnings per share is $10. Therefore, the company's P/E ratio is 10.

You can find a public company's P/E ratio listed in the financial pages of newspapers, along with the stock price and daily trading volume. The P/E ratio printed there is based on last year's reported earnings. This is called a trailing P/E. A professional stock analyst may use a forward P/E, based on his or her forecast of next year's earnings. That's why you see a company's stock price rise or fall immediately after the company announces its predictions of its next quarter's earnings.

If you look at the column of P/E ratios in the financial pages, you will notice a wide range of numbers. A high P/E ratio suggests that investors expect high earnings growth for the stock. A low P/E ratio could mean a number of different things, such as:

- ◆ The company is in a mature, low-growth industry.

- ◆ The company's business is sensitive to a temporary economic downturn.

- ◆ The company is experiencing serious financial difficulties.

BULL$ 'N' BEAR$ reprinted by permission of United Feature Syndicate, Inc.

P/E ratios are also calculated for stock market benchmarks such as the Standard & Poor's 500 index. A review of historic P/E ratios for the S&P 500 shows marked variation from year to year. For example, the year-end S&P 500 P/E ratio climbed from 10.4 in 1984 to 31.3 in

1999. Did investors in 1999 expect more earnings growth than investors in 1984? Or were the 1999 investors overly optimistic and buying on speculation?

By the way, most professional stock analysts profess to use fundamental analysis. There aren't too many investment industry jobs offered to individuals who admit to being irrational.

Will the real earnings please stand up?

Typically, investors consider a company's recent reported earnings as one factor in forecasting future earnings. To keep reported earnings looking good, many companies take advantage of the flexibility built into accounting rules. Some companies push the limits—or ignore them all together. That's why federal law requires that independent accounting firms audit reported financial results of public companies.

The job of an independent auditor is to keep a sharp eye on what the company is doing. So, what about Enron's auditor?

For years, Enron was audited by Arthur Andersen, once one of the most respected accounting firms in the world. When the head of Arthur Andersen, Joseph F. Berardino, testified before Congress in December 2001, he said the crucial transaction that led to Enron's collapse involved only $5.7 million. He also testified that, in addition, Enron had overstated stockholders' equity by $172 million. But the $172 million was just a "small item" that fell outside the scope of an audit of a company of Enron's size. *The New York Times* asked: How can $172 million be small when $5.7 million is crucial?

For months into the Enron post-mortem period, Arthur Andersen tried to distance itself from Enron's accounting scandal. But first the firm publicly admitted that its personnel had shredded literally tons of potentially key Enron audit documents. Later the firm portrayed the shredding as the work of "rogue" personnel in Andersen's

Houston office. Nevertheless, in March 2002, a federal grand jury indicted the entire firm of Arthur Andersen for obstruction of justice.

According to an Arthur Andersen spokesperson, the indictment was "without precedent and an extraordinary abuse of prosecutorial discretion." However, in just the few years prior to the Enron collapse, Arthur Andersen had paid some of the largest legal settlements ever to shareholders and others who sued because of Andersen's audit failures. In June 2000, Andersen paid several million dollars in fines to the Securities and Exchange Commission (SEC).

After a four-week trial in the obstruction of justice case, a jury found the firm guilty of the charge. The conviction cost Arthur Andersen its ability to audit public companies. Within months, the firm was effectively out of business.

It wasn't just clients of Arthur Andersen that experienced accounting lapses in the 1990s. Between 1997 and 2000, more than 700 companies found significant mistakes in their past financial statements and had to restate their earnings—downward. That's very unusual. In 1981, only three companies restated their reported earnings.

Arthur Levitt, who served as SEC chairman during the Clinton administration, wrote the following about abusive accounting practices during his tenure in his 2002 book *Take on the Street* (see the Bibliography for publication information):

> *Corporations were playing with the earnings calculation until they arrived at the best possible number. Earnings press releases revealed only the good news—or those details that helped boost the share price. Auditors, increasingly captive of their clients, would give them the clean audits they wanted, despite lots of chicanery. Consulting fees—for everything from information technology design and installation to management compensation and merger analysis—were pouring in. Audit fees made up 70 percent of account firm revenues in 1976 but only 31 percent in 1998. More and more, it became clear that*

the auditors didn't want to do anything to rock the boat with clients, potentially jeopardizing their chief source of income. Consulting contracts were turning accounting firms into extensions of management—even cheerleaders at times. Some firms even paid their auditors on how many nonaudit services they sold to their clients.

In July 2002, President George W. Bush signed an accounting industry reform law called the Sarbanes-Oxley Act. The law forbids a public accounting firm from auditing a client company at the same time that it provides certain non-audit services to that client.

The Sarbanes-Oxley Act also requires the chief executive officer (CEO) and chief financial officer (CFO) of each public company to certify the financial results in each quarterly and annual report. The potential penalties for lying in earnings reports or to the SEC are up to $5 million in fines and up to 20 years in prison.

In addition, the CEO and CFO are on the hook if their company has to restate prior earnings because of accounting misconduct. The CEO and CFO must reimburse the company for any bonus or other incentive compensation they received during the 12-month period after the misstated financial report was filed with the SEC or issued to the public.

At the bill-signing ceremony at the White House, President Bush touted the Sarbanes-Oxley Act as the most important investor protection law since the 1930s. Does that mean all the problems are solved? Far from it!

In October 2002, the U.S. General Accounting Office (GAO) announced that 10 percent of public companies had restated their earnings due to accounting errors at least once during the prior five years. And the GAO suggested that the worst is yet to come.

These earnings restatements mean billions of dollars of lost market value for investors who bought stock based on false information.

If you are an investor who pays attention to corporate earnings, you may have good reason to mistrust earnings reports in general, at least those from the pre–Sarbanes-Oxley era. If you would have used those earnings reports to help predict a company's future prospects, you now may have less information to help you decide what a stock may be worth.

Moreover, because of the threat of Sarbanes-Oxley penalties, corporate accounting practices in the near future are likely to be more conservative than ever. Don't be surprised to see a sharp drop in reported earnings. You may still be asking: Will the real earnings please stand up?

Potential earnings restatements may be enough to make you question the "E" in P/E. Unfortunately, there is more bad news. The effects of potential pension-fund adjustments may be just around the corner.

You might think that the ups and downs of the investments in a company's traditional pension fund have no effect on the company's income statement for its business operations. Guess again.

A public company that offers a traditional pension plan to its employees must set aside enough money in its pension fund to pay the pensions of current and future retirees. The typical pension plan invests 60 to 65 percent of this money in the stock market.

When the stock investments in its pension fund are doing great, the company doesn't have to set aside more money. However, when the pension fund becomes underfunded because of stock market losses, the company has to add more money to the pot.

Meeting these pension obligations reduces the amount that the company could pay in dividends or reinvest in the business. Contributing to a pension fund is an expense that reduces earnings.

If this line of analysis sounds as though it's going in a circle, you're right. As corporate earnings fall, stock prices fall. As stock prices fall, corporate pension funds become underfunded. As corporate pension funds become underfunded, companies have to put more money into the funds, which reduces earnings. Corporate earnings fall, stock prices fall. Circle complete.

According to a 2002 Credit Suisse First Boston study, more than 70 percent of the 500 companies that make up the Standard & Poor's 500 have traditional pension obligations. Of these pension-obligated companies, about 90 percent had underfunded pension funds at the end of 2002. For some of these companies, the necessary pension fund contributions may be just enough to put them into bankruptcy.

Conventional investment advice

Listen to the mutual fund industry:

- ◆ Historically, long-term stock market investments have outperformed other investment choices.
- ◆ Taking risks is essential to a comfortable retirement.
- ◆ Market timing doesn't work.
- ◆ Stay the course.

This may be good advice. It may have served many individuals in the past. It may or may not be good advice for you today. But if enough 401(k) investors take this advice, it will definitely be good for the mutual fund industry.

Mutual fund companies make their money from management fees. These fees are usually based on a percentage of the assets under their management. The more 401(k) money that goes into mutual funds—and stays there—the better it is for the mutual fund industry.

Perhaps more significantly, the entire stock market needs the inertia of 401(k) investors to help keep it steady. According to *The Wall Street Journal* article "What Stock Investors Need: First, Trust in Firms' Numbers" (July 17, 2002), "For all the things pushing down on stocks, there's one important change that's helping cushion the decline: an unceasing stream of investments into stock mutual funds through

401(k) plans." The page-one article called that "good news." And it called signs of a few 401(k) investors pulling out of stock funds as "troubling" for the stock market.

After experiencing the biggest losses since the Great Depression, some investors think that this is more than a conventional bear market. And they have some doubts about conventional investment advice.

Key Points About Asset Allocation

◆ Subtract your age from 100 percent and put the resulting percentage (or less) of your 401(k) money into the stock market.

◆ There's no guarantee that stocks will outperform other investment vehicles over the next 20 years.

◆ Stocks are worth what investors are willing to pay for them.

◆ A rational approach to investing in stocks emphasizes corporate earnings.

◆ Recent accounting scandals have caused a crisis of confidence in reported earnings.

◆ Underfunded corporate pension funds may be a looming problem for the affected companies and their shareholders.

◆ Consider the advice of the investment community but think for yourself, too.

Chapter 2

Minimizing the Downside Risk of Employer Stock

"Employees who have worked hard and saved all their lives should not have to risk losing everything if their company fails."

—President George W. Bush, February 2, 2002

T HE COLLAPSE OF ENRON REVEALED TO many Americans for the first time the risk associated with employees' heavy investment in their employers' stock. Employee investment in employer stock is very common. Over the past five years, the percentage of assets in 401(k) plans in employer stock has held steady at about 19 percent. That is significantly higher than the 10-percent limit that many financial planners recommend.

Enron's 401(k) plan had nearly 58 percent of its total assets in Enron stock (according to DC Plan Investing newsletter). That's not unusual, especially among large public companies.

In 2001, three companies had more than 90 percent of 401(k) assets invested in employer stock: Proctor & Gamble, with 92 percent; Sherwin-Williams, with 92 percent; and Abbott Laboratories, with 90 percent. Coca-Cola had 81 percent of its plan assets in employer stock, Texas Instruments had 76 percent, and McDonald's had 74 percent (according to DC Plan Investing newsletter). About 2,000 American employers have 401(k) plans that are heavily invested in their own stock, according to the Employee Benefit Research Institute (EBRI).

Large company 401(k) plans are more likely than small company plans to offer employer stock, according to "Company Stock in 401(k) Plans," a 2002 EBRI report. Large 401(k) plans are also more likely to require that employer matching contributions be invested in employer stock. In some 43 percent of those plans that offer employer stock as an investment alternative, employers require that matching contributions be invested in employer stock.

Most companies that use their own stock as matching contributions to employees' accounts restrict the employees' ability to sell the stock and invest the proceeds in other investment alternatives. Among the companies that impose transfer restrictions on employer stock, more than half (60 percent) have a restriction that is based on the employee's age and/or the number of years the employee has worked for the company. And 27 percent of employers apply restrictions throughout a participant's investment in the plan. Just 13 percent have no such restrictions. Only 14 percent of plans limit the percentage of employer stock a participant may hold in his or her 401(k) account.

Employers that have traditional pension plans as well as 401(k) plans are more likely to also offer employer stock as an investment alternative in the 401(k) plan. Such employers are also more likely to require that 401(k) plan participants invest in employer stock. They are also more likely to impose restrictions on selling that stock.

What's so terrible about employer stock?

Heavy investment in employer stock is risky. It's that simple.

Even if your employer doesn't go bankrupt as Enron did, the long-term impact of holding a significant amount of your employer's stock may be to lower your living standard in retirement.

A recent analysis found that two out of three companies that use employer stock as their matching contribution provided a lower investment return than the S&P 500 index, the most widely used investment benchmark. The S&P 500 index is more stable than the price of almost any individual stock. Because it is a composite of many companies, it is much less volatile than an individual stock.

Studies have shown that, over the years, measurements of overall stock market volatility have stayed relatively constant. But over the past three decades, individual stock volatility has more than doubled.

So, for the 401(k) account owner who invests heavily in his or her employer's stock—an individual stock—risk is increased and expected return is reduced. That's the opposite of what you should do when you invest.

Clearly, an employee who holds 100-percent employer stock in a 401(k) account bears more risk than if he or she held a well-diversified investment portfolio. This means that the odds are against you profiting by putting a large percentage of your 401(k) money in your employer's stock.

Holding a significant amount of employer stock in a 401(k) account is so risky that some observers refer to it as a form of gambling. It's risky enough even if the employer does not go bankrupt, but, as Enron employees learned the hard way, the situation gets worse after bankruptcy.

In recent years, public companies have been filing for bankruptcies at a record pace. Companies that recently filed for bankruptcy include United Airlines, WorldCom, and Global Crossing.

The corporate bankruptcy trend is expected to continue over the next couple of years. That doesn't bode well for employees of those companies, especially if they are invested in employer stock.

Unlike 401(k) plans, traditional pensions are generally guaranteed by the federal government if the employer goes bankrupt. If you work for a company that provides a traditional pension as well as a 401(k) plan, the stability of that monthly income for life offsets some of the risk of employer stock in your 401(k) plan. That's because the pension plan acts as a guaranteed annuity among your total retirement assets.

However, having only one company's stock in a 401(k) account creates a risk level that is almost impossible to offset. For most individuals, it will mean less money in retirement.

If you work for a company that provides both a traditional pension and a 401(k) plan, employer stock could be considered a calculated risk—something you do with a small part of your total retirement savings. However, if your retirement savings consist of 401(k) assets only, employer stock is very risky.

What's so great about employer stock?

Companies claim that employee investment in the company encourages employee loyalty by aligning workers' interests with the company's. Whether or not that really happens is debatable, but the effect of the practice on the company's bottom line is unmistakable. Here's what takes place.

Making matching contributions to 401(k) accounts in the form of stock allows companies to reward employees without spending any cash. (When employees leave the company, they may sell their stock in the stock market for cash.) Moreover, companies save taxes at the same time because the contributions of employer stock are tax-deductible as an employee benefit expense. There aren't too many tax deductions a corporation can take without spending any cash. This is potentially a big one.

In the volatile stock markets of the 1990s, many companies discovered another corporate advantage of heavy employee ownership in the company's stock: It helps stabilize a company's stock price. That's because 401(k) account owners tend to be long-term investors—that is, they buy and hold. Companies may even impose restrictions on selling the stock to ensure that a large block of stock does not trade in the market.

Some observers assert that today's employers are using employees' stock ownership in 401(k) plans as a strategy to manipulate the price of the stock. This was not the intended purpose of the laws that allow—even encourage—employee ownership of employer stock. Such a corporate practice may even violate the employer's fiduciary duty—that is, its obligation to run the 401(k) plan in the best interests of the participants.

With so many reasons to avoid heavy investment in employer stock, why do so many individuals do it? Some hold employer stock because that is what their employers use to match the employees' contributions to the plan. Essentially, they have no choice. Even if the employer stock is a risky investment, getting the stock may be better than getting nothing at all.

"My 401(k) is safe. It's tied up in booze futures."

Some employers offer incentives for employees to invest their 401(k) contributions in its stock. For example, your employer may offer its stock at a price that is lower than the current market price. Or you may be able to contribute a higher percentage of your pay if you choose employer stock. And in certain instances, the amount you choose to invest in employer stock can determine the percentage of the match you receive.

Investing in your employer's stock also may seem to be a smart decision. After all, you know its products and services better than most investors do. You may know about the strength of the company's management and the company's plans to expand the business. These are indeed some of the factors you should consider when you invest in any company's stock.

Tax advantages provide another reason to invest in employer stock. If you own employer stock that has appreciated in value while you held it in your 401(k) account, you may have an attractive tax savings opportunity when you retire. If you take a lump-sum distribution from the plan, you will not, in most cases, be taxed at regular income tax rates on the stock's appreciation.

Usually, all taxable distributions from a qualified plan are taxed as regular income. But with employer stock, you can pay lower capital gains tax rates on this appreciation when you eventually sell the stock. (For more details and examples, see Appendix B.)

In spite of all these good reasons to invest heavily in employer stock, remember that you already depend on your employer for your salary. You might want to think hard about linking your financial security in retirement to the same source as your financial security today. If your employer goes out of business, you would lose both your job and your retirement savings.

Reducing your employer stock holdings

Employees who want to reduce their dependence on employer stock need to understand the other investment alternatives in their

401(k) plan and how their particular plan works. Every 401(k) plan is unique. Although each 401(k) plan must meet certain federal standards and file financial reports with the federal government, each employer sets many of the rules for its plan—including investment alternatives, limitations on plan participant contributions, the company's formula for matching plan participant contributions, and loan and withdrawal options.

To reduce your employer stock holdings, you need to find out how your plan works. How do you get started? First, pull together all the information you can about your plan. You are entitled to a plain-English document called a summary plan description (SPD) that describes your plan's features. You may also have Internet access to information about your company's plan. Ask your human resources department for help in gathering the available information.

Once you have the SPD, it should help you answer some key questions. Does your employer match a portion of your contributions to the plan? If it does, is the match in employer stock? Are you restricted on what you can do with that stock? How can you change your investment holdings? What are your investment alternatives?

Your SPD explains:

◆ Your eligibility to participate in your employer's 401(k) plan.

◆ The vesting schedule for your employer's contributions.

◆ Your maximum annual contribution (as a dollar amount and as a percentage of your pay).

◆ The formula for your employer's matching contributions.

◆ The procedures for taking out your money when you leave your employer.

◆ Your rights under the Employee Retirement Income Security Act (ERISA).

If your 401(k) account is heavily invested in employer stock, what should you do? Diversify—that is, put your money into several different investment alternatives. Diversification is critical, particularly when your 401(k) account will be your only source of retirement income.

Keep employer stock to a small fraction of your investments, no more than 10 percent. This recommended percentage is based on years of research that shows that investment risk is significantly reduced by dividing an investment portfolio evenly into 10 or more randomly selected investments. If your employer's match is in its own stock, diversify by putting your own contributions somewhere else, such as in a stock index fund, bond fund, or a stable value investment.

If your employer's matching contribution is in its stock and you are not allowed to sell it—similar to the situation many Enron workers faced—there may not be much that you can do. Keep checking your employer's policy, though. In the wake of Enron, many employers are voluntarily loosening their restrictions regarding employer stock in their employees' 401(k) accounts.

Allocate your 401(k) investment portfolio based on your age and tolerance for risk. If you are younger than 35, you may be able to afford to invest most of your savings in the stock market because, if it goes down, you have time to wait for it to recover. If you are older, consider allocating more to stable value investments. Alternatively, split your contributions between a stock and bond fund.

If you are retired, or near retirement, consider easing off on stocks—but don't get out of the stock market entirely. Even if you're 65 now, you could live another 30 years or more. In that case, you'll need your retirement savings to grow.

Make sure that you occasionally rebalance your investments. If you decide that you should be 50 percent in stocks and 50 percent in a money market fund, and the value of your money market fund has shot up to be 80 percent of your investment portfolio, it may be time to shift some funds to stocks. That process may have the effect of making you buy stocks when prices are low.

You might also want to consider increasing the amount of money you are saving that isn't connected to your employer or your 401(k) plan. If you have a Roth IRA as well, you won't get a tax deduction now, but you will have more control over how those funds are invested. (See discussion of Roth IRAs on pages 47-49 and pages 90-91.)

Key Questions to Ask About Employer Stock in Your 401(k) Account

- ♦ What is the value of my 401(k) account?
- ♦ What is the value of employer stock in my 401(k) account?
- ♦ Is the value of employer stock more than 10 percent of the total value of my account?
- ♦ Can I move some of my 401(k) money out of employer stock and into a different investment alternative?
- ♦ How risky is each of the investment alternatives?
- ♦ How much risk can I be comfortable with?
- ♦ Considering my age and years to retirement, how much risk can I afford?
- ♦ What do I have to do to move 401(k) funds into a different investment alternative?

Chapter 3

Saving More for Your Retirement

"Every man and every woman should lay up some portion of their income, whether that income be great or small."

—*The American Frugal Housewife*, Twelfth Edition, by Mrs. Child, 1832

I F YOU ARE STILL WORKING AND accumulating money in your 401(k) account, asset allocation and diversification concepts are just as important for you as for retirees. But as a pre-retiree, you have two additional issues to consider: how much to save and whether to save all of it in a 401(k) plan.

In the 1990s, contributing to a 401(k) plan was often promoted as a way to build a nest egg so that you would be able to retire at an early age. In the first three years of the new millennium, though, the labor force participation of workers aged 55 to 64 actually increased by 2 percentage points. Why? No one can say for sure, but experts believe that the steep drop in the value of 401(k) accounts during this period forced many young retirees to go back to work.

In 2000, the average total value of retirement accounts (401(k), IRA, and others) owned by pre-retirees aged 55 to 64 was not very healthy. The mean value of the accounts held by these pre-retirees was only $71,910. For a 65-year-old who retired in December 2002, that amount would buy a level, single-life annuity that paid only $515 per month. Americans' personal savings rate has steadily declined over the past three decades, as you can see in Figure 3-1. If you have "typical" American saving habits, you may need to save more each year in order to retire comfortably.

Are you losing hope about retirement? If so, that's understand-able. Just try not to give up and stop saving. Contributing to a 401(k)

Figure 3-1. Personal Income and Personal Savings, 1960–2001

Amounts in billions

Year	Disposable personal income*	Personal savings**	Savings rate***
1960	$366.2	$26.2	7.2%
1965	498.9	42.7	8.6%
1970	736.5	69.5	9.4%
1975	1,181.4	125.2	10.6%
1980	2,019.8	205.6	10.2%
1985	3,086.5	282.6	9.2%
1990	4,293.6	334.3	7.8%
1995	5,422.6	302.4	5.6%
1996	5,677.7	272.1	4.8%
1997	5,968.2	252.9	4.2%
1998	6,355.6	301.5	4.7%
1999	6,618.0	160.9	2.4%
2000	7,120.2	201.5	2.8%
2001	7,393.2	169.7	2.3%

Source: Congressional Research Service.

* Personal income minus taxes and non-tax payments.

** Disposable personal income minus personal consumption expenditures, interest payments, and personal transfers to persons outside the United States.

*** Personal savings divided by disposable personal income.

plan is still important, especially if your employer matches your contributions or if you have a high income. But for reasons explained later, consider alternative ways to save money for your retirement.

If you're like most American workers, you're just not saving enough. In recent years, the personal savings rate has steadily declined. In the late 1970s, the American savings rate was more than 10 percent. In 2001, it was only 2.3 percent. That's not nearly enough for a comfortable retirement. Figure 3-2 shows that the average American's retirement savings are inadequate to support living costs in later years without earned income.

Figure 3-2. Retirement Account Balances* of Workers** in 2000, by Age

Age of worker	Mean*** account value	Median**** account value
25 to 34 years old	$14,780	$6,000
35 to 44 years old	$41,050	$19,500
45 to 54 years old	$60,740	$28,000
55 to 64 years old	$71,910	$33,000
Total: 25 to 64 years old	$45,960	$18,000

Source: Congressional Research Service.

* Includes IRAs, 401(k)-type accounts, and Keogh accounts for self-employed individuals.

** Includes employed individuals who own at least one retirement account. Does not include approximately 65.5 million employed individuals who did not own any type of retirement account.

*** Mean is a simple arithmetic average that is calculated by adding up the reported values of all accounts and dividing this total by the number of account-holders. As a measure of "average," the mean is flawed because it can be biased by a relatively small number of unusually high or low values.

**** Median is calculated by ordering all of the observed values from highest to lowest and finding the value that lies exactly at the midpoint. This measure of average is more representative of the population because it is not biased by unusually high or low values.

How much to save

In 2003, you can contribute up to $12,000 of your pay to your employer's 401(k) on a pre-tax basis, and up to $14,000 if you are age 50 or older. These maximum contribution amounts are scheduled to increase as follows:

	Younger Than Age 50	Age 50 or Older
2004	$13,000	$16,000
2006-2007	$14,000	$18,000
2008	$15,000	$20,000

Your employer may also limit your contribution to a certain percentage of your pay. Up to these dollar amount and percentage limits, the amount you actually contribute to your 401(k) is up to you. How should you decide what that contribution amount should be?

On the Internet you may find many retirement savings calculators that ask you how much 401(k) money you want to have when you retire, how many years until you retire, and the average annual investment return that you expect to enjoy. Plug in that data and the monthly contribution that you need to make spits out. Typically, the result is depressing.

The typical retirement savings calculator is flawed for one or more of the following reasons:

- ◆ It relies on a constant rate of return.
- ◆ It relies on a constant rate of inflation.
- ◆ It ignores the possibility of deflation.
- ◆ It assumes you will live only as long as a mortality table says you will.

A more sophisticated retirement planning tool called "Monte Carlo" simulation uses randomness to help predict adequate retirement savings. To generate 401(k) investment advice, a Monte Carlo simulation posits thousands of realistic possibilities for unpredictable future conditions, such as inflation, interest rates, and stock market returns. Then, Monte Carlo analysis uses statistical theory to present the size of an individual's future retirement savings portfolio as a range of possible amounts. So, a Monte Carlo analysis might tell you that saving $12,000 a year in your 401(k) over the next 20 years would give you a 99-percent chance of retiring with at least $240,000 and a 10-percent chance of retiring with at least one million dollars.

Offering Monte Carlo simulation is the latest trend in the offices of financial advisors—and even a few Internet retirement calculators. However, many individuals who have used Monte Carlo simulation have found the exercise confusing. A realistic and understandable shortcut to determining your annual savings goal may simply be 10 percent of your annual gross income—at a minimum. The tougher question is where to put that 10 percent.

401(k) tax trap

The traditional lure of 401(k) investing has been the opportunity to reduce current federal and state income taxes. These taxes are deferred for the portion of your pay that you contribute to a 401(k) plan. Of course, you pay taxes on your withdrawals from the 401(k) plans.

That's the catch. And these days, the tax deferral may no longer be a good reason to contribute pre-tax dollars to a 401(k) plan.

You might think that saving in a 401(k) plan reduces your total taxes over your lifetime. That might be true if you take your money out of your 401(k) plan when you are in a lower tax bracket than when you put the money in.

However, if you withdraw money from your 401(k) account after tax rates increase, you may increase the total taxes you pay over your lifetime. This is especially true for low- and middle-income individuals, according to a 2001 study by economist and economics professor

Laurence Kotlikoff and economists Jagadeesh Gokhale and Todd Neumann.

According to this study, a low- or moderate-income household generally raises its lifetime taxes and lowers its lifetime expenditures by enthusiastic saving in a 401(k) account with an 8-percent real return on assets. That's because Social Security benefits are taxed at low- to mid-income levels. The household's movement into a higher tax bracket or increased tax rates overall would raise the household's lifetime taxes and reduce its lifetime expenditures even more.

> **Example.** A typical married couple with $50,000 annual earnings takes full advantage of a typical 401(k) plan instead of putting the same amount of savings into after-tax investments. Using the 401(k) plan during a stable tax rate period raises their lifetime taxes by 6.4 percent and reduces their lifetime spending by 1.7 percent. If the couple's marginal tax rate increases by 20 percent when the couple retires, lifetime taxes increase by 7.3 percent and lifetime spending decreases by 2.3 percent.

For a high-income household, 401(k) plan participation in a stable tax rate period does not generally increase lifetime taxes. Such a household pays the highest taxes on Social Security benefits regardless of any withdrawals from its tax-deferred savings accounts.

> **Example.** A married couple with a $300,000 annual income maxes out its 401(k) savings opportunity. The investments in the couple's 401(k) account have an average return of 6 percent. If tax rates are stable, the couple reaps a 6.7 percent lifetime tax break and a 3.8 percent increase in lifetime spending.

However, even a high-income household would increase its lifetime taxes if it withdrew 401(k) money during a period of significantly higher tax rates. So, 401(k) plans and other retirement savings strategies that rely on tax deferral don't always make sense. Tax deferral is counter-productive for an individual if tax rates will be higher during that individual's retirement years.

Federal income tax rates are at historically low levels, as Figure 3-3 indicates. Growing federal government budget deficits and Social Security program funding requirements are likely to put upward pressure on tax rates in the future.

Figure 3-3. The History of Federal Individual Income Tax Rates

Calendar year	Highest tax rate*	Calendar year	Highest tax rate*
1913	7%	1937	79%
1914	7%	1938	79%
1915	7%	1939	79%
1916	15%	1940	81.1%
1917	67%	1941	81%
1918	77%	1942	88%
1919	73%	1943	88%
1920	73%	1944	94%
1921	73%	1945	94%
1922	56%	1946	86.45%
1923	56%	1947	86.45%
1924	46%	1948	82.13%
1925	25%	1949	82.13%
1926	25%	1950	91%
1927	25%	1951	91%
1928	25%	1952	92%
1929	24%	1953	92%
1930	25%	1954	91%
1931	25%	1955	91%
1932	63%	1956	91%
1933	63%	1957	91%
1934	63%	1958	91%
1935	63%	1959	91%
1936	79%	1960	91%

(continued on next page)

Figure 3-3. The History of Federal Individual Income Tax Rates (cont'd.)

Calendar year	Highest tax rate*	Calendar year	Highest tax rate*
1961	91%	1984	50%
1962	91%	1985	50%
1963	91%	1986	50%
1964	77%	1987	38.5%
1965	70%	1988	28%
1966	70%	1989	28%
1967	70%	1990	28%
1968	75.25	1991	31%
1969	77%	1992	31%
1970	71.75	1993	39.6%
1971	70%	1994	39.6%
1972	70%	1995	39.6%
1973	70%	1996	39.6%
1974	70%	1997	39.6%
1975	70%	1998	39.6%
1976	70%	1999	39.6%
1977	70%	2000	39.6%
1978	70%	2001	38.6%
1979	70%	2002	38.6%
1980	70%	2003	38.6%
1981	69.125%	2004	37.6%
1982	50%	2005	37.6%
1983	50%	2006	35%

Source: Congressional Joint Committee on Taxation and the Internal Revenue Code.

* For highest income bracket.

We can expect state income taxes to increase as well. Many state governments are struggling with some of the worst gaps between revenue and spending since World War II. The budget problems are largely due to the following:

- ◆ Exploding healthcare costs.

- ◆ Deteriorating state tax collection systems.

- ◆ Lost tax revenue due to a sluggish economy.

- ◆ Homeland security expenses.

The likelihood of tax rate increases begs the following question: Why should you continue to contribute to your employer's 401(k) plan? The answer: your employer's matching contribution and a federal tax credit for contributions to qualifying retirement accounts.

An employer's matching contribution to an employee's 401(k) account is a common employee benefit. In a survey of companies with 401(k) plans conducted in 2002 by the Ayco Company, 94 percent of the companies matched their employees' contributions. The most common employer matching formula is a match equal to 50 percent of the first 6 percent of an employee's pay contributed to his or her 401(k) account.

> **Example.** Rhonda's annual salary is $30,000. She contributes 6 percent of her salary to her 401(k) account each year and her employer matches 50 percent of her contribution. Therefore, Rhonda contributes $1,800 to her 401(k) account this year (6% x $30,000). Her employer contributes $900 to her account this year (50% x $1,800).

According to the Kotlikoff-Gokhale-Neuman study, the benefit of the typical 50-percent employer match exceeds the employee's lifetime tax increase triggered by 401(k) plan participation. However, in early 2003, some companies were forced to abandon their matching programs because of the cost.

Low- and middle-income savers may also benefit from a federal tax credit that is available through 2006. The federal tax law provides a nonrefundable tax credit (a direct offset against tax) for part of the contributions eligible individuals make to qualifying retirement accounts.

To be eligible for the credit, you must be age 18 or older and not a full-time student or a dependent claimed on someone else's tax return. The credit is available in addition to any deduction or exclusion that is otherwise available for your contribution.

The maximum annual contribution eligible for the credit is $2,000. The credit percentage rate ranges from 50 percent to 0, depending on your filing status and adjusted gross income (AGI). (See the following chart, with information provided by the Internal Revenue Code.)

Credit Rate	Married-Joint AGI	Head of Household AGI	Single/Other AGI
50%	$0–30,000	$0–22,500	$0–15,000
20%	$30,001–32,500	$22,501–24,375	$15,001–16,250
10%	$32,501–50,000	$24,376–37,500	$16,251–25,000
0%	More than $50,000	More than $37,500	More than $25,000

Contributions that qualify for this tax credit include not only your contributions to 401(k) accounts, but also your contributions to traditional individual retirement accounts (IRAs) and Roth IRAs. So if you are going to contribute at least $2,000 to an IRA in the same year that you contribute to your 401(k) account, you won't get more of a tax benefit from your 401(k) account contribution. Once you contribute to your 401(k) plan account up to the amount that your employer will match, you should consider stashing your annual retirement savings in another investment vehicle.

Other retirement investments

Many individuals say that they like the convenience of automatic and regular deductions from their pay to contribute to their 401(k) accounts. And they claim that they will not regularly and consistently invest their take-home pay that is increased by limiting their 401(k) contributions to the employer match.

However, an automatic withdrawal of Roth IRA contributions from a checking or savings account may work just as nicely as automatic 401(k) deduction from a paycheck. And beginning in 2003, the tax law allows employers to add a "deemed IRA" feature to their 401(k) plans and deduct Roth IRA contributions directly from employees' paychecks. Ask your employer's human resources department or payroll department if your employer offers a deemed IRA feature.

Saving money in a Roth IRA eliminates the risk that retirement withdrawals will be taxed at higher tax rates. Withdrawals of Roth IRA contribution amounts (but not Roth IRA conversion amounts) are always tax-free. Withdrawals of Roth IRA earnings are tax-free if certain requirements are met.

Generally, to avoid paying taxes and penalties on Roth IRA earnings, you must keep all the earnings in the Roth IRA account for at least five years. At that point, withdrawals of earnings are tax free if you:

- Are age 59½ or older.
- Are disabled.
- Have died and your beneficiaries are withdrawing money.
- Are using up to $10,000 of Roth IRA earnings for home-buying expenses of a first-time homebuyer.

In 2003 and 2004, an eligible individual may contribute up to $3,000 to a Roth IRA, and up to $3,500 if he or she is age 50 or older. These maximum contribution amounts are scheduled to increase as follows:

	Younger Than Age 50	Age 50 or Older
2005	$4,000	$4,500
2006–2007	$4,000	$5,000
2008	$5,000	$6,000

Eligibility to contribute to a Roth IRA is based on earned income. For example, individuals who earn $3,000 in compensation may contribute up to $3,000 to a Roth IRA. A married couple may contribute as much as $6,000 ($3,000 for each spouse), even if one spouse does not work, as long as the couple's joint compensation is at least $6,000.

The maximum Roth IRA contributions are phased out as AGI rises from $95,000 to $110,000 (unmarried), $150,000 to $160,000 (married filing a joint tax return), and $0 to $10,000 (married filing a separate tax return). If you already have a traditional IRA, you can convert it to a Roth IRA if (1) your modified adjusted gross income does not exceed $100,000, and (2) you file a joint return if you are married. (For more information on Roth IRA conversions, see pages 90-91 and page 105.)

If you have a Roth IRA, you'll face the same investment issues you have with your 401(k): asset allocation, risk tolerance, and diversification. But with a Roth IRA (other than a deemed Roth IRA), you'll have one investment option that's not available for 401(k) plans: a bank account.

Unlike money market mutual funds, bank accounts are insured by the federal government, up to total deposits of $100,000 per bank. And these days, some bank accounts are offering significantly better returns than most money-market mutual funds.

Interest paid on money-market mutual funds has decreased dramatically as the Federal Reserve Bank (the Fed) has cut its interest rates. In contrast, bank account interest rates are not as closely tied to the Fed's activities. Bank rates depend more on banks' business strategies and the interest rates that the banks impose on their loans.

Once you've maxed out on your Roth IRA, or you're not eligible to contribute because of income limitations, you may want to consider investing your savings in taxable investment vehicles, such as bank certificates of deposit, investment-grade gold coins (which are volatile in price), and U.S. Treasury securities.

U.S. Treasury securities are debt obligations of the federal government. They are a safe and secure investment option because the full faith and credit of the United States government guarantees that interest and principal payments will be paid on time.

You can buy treasuries from a financial institution, broker, or dealer—or directly from the government by visiting the Website *www.publicdebt.treas.gov* or calling 1-800-722-2678. Generally, interest income on Treasury securities is taxable for federal income tax purposes but is not taxable for state or local income tax purposes.

Treasury securities available to individual investors include treasury bills, treasury notes, treasury bonds, and U.S. savings bonds. Most Treasury securities (but not U.S. savings bonds) are liquid, which means they can easily be sold for cash. You can buy Treasury bills, notes, and bonds for a minimum of $1,000, and you can buy savings bonds for as little as $25.

Treasury bills (or T-bills) are short-term securities that mature in one year or less from their issue date. You buy T-bills for a price less than their par (face) value. When they mature, the U.S. Treasury pays you their par value. Your interest is the difference between the purchase price of the security and what the Treasury pays you at maturity (or what you get if you sell the bill before it matures).

> **Example.** If you bought a $10,000 26-week Treasury bill for $9,750 and held it until maturity, your interest would be $250.

Treasury notes and bonds are securities that pay a fixed rate of interest every six months until your security matures, which is when the federal government pays you their par value. The only difference between notes and bonds is the number of years until maturity. Treasury notes mature in more than a year, but not more than 10 years from their issue date. Bonds, on the other hand, mature in more than 10 years from their issue date. You usually can buy notes and bonds for a price close to their par value.

The U.S. Treasury sells two kinds of notes and bonds: fixed-principal and inflation-indexed. Both pay interest twice a year, but the principal value of inflation-indexed securities is adjusted to reflect inflation as measured by the Consumer Price Index. With inflation-indexed notes and bonds, your semiannual interest payments and maturity payment are based on the inflation-adjusted principal value of your security.

Think like a millionaire

Americans can't count on the stock market to provide them with comfortable retirement years. As the average 401(k) account gets smaller and 401(k) account owners live longer, it becomes clearer that Americans must simply save more for retirement.

Although you can't control the stock market, you can control your spending. One way to control your spending is to start thinking like a millionaire.

Dr. Thomas J. Stanley, author of *The Millionaire Mind*, writes that the most important thing he has learned from studying millionaires is that "you cannot enjoy life if you are addicted to consumption and the use of credit." According to Dr. Stanley, typical millionaires accumulate substantial wealth in part because they are frugal.

Common money-saving habits of millionaires include shopping with coupons, switching long-distance telephone companies, and having old shoes resoled. If such habits work for millionaires, they can work for you, too.

How to Save More for Your Retirement

- Every year, save at least 10 percent of your gross income for your retirement.

- Because tax deferral strategies don't make sense if the tax rates are going to rise, contribute to your 401(k) only up to the amount that your employer will match.

- Unlike 401(k) account distributions, Roth IRA distributions are tax-free, if certain requirements are met.

- Consider investing some of your retirement savings directly in U.S. Treasury securities and holding the Treasuries until maturity.

Chapter 4

Watching Out for Employer Misconduct

*"The time to guard against corruption and tyranny is before they
shall have gotten hold of us. It is better to keep the wolf
out of the fold than to trust to drawing his teeth and talons
after he shall have entered."*

—Thomas Jefferson

THE ACCOUNTING GAMES ENRON PLAYED HELPED support the price
of its stock—until the truth came out. But before the rest of the
world knew what was really happening at Enron, the company's executives and other insiders received $1.3 billion between 1999 and
mid-2001 by exercising their stock options and selling their Enron
stock. In contrast, more than 14,000 rank-and-file Enron employees
who participated in Enron's 401(k) retirement plan saw much of their
retirement savings evaporate because their 401(k) accounts were heavily
concentrated in Enron stock.

On September 26, 2001, Enron Corporation's chairman, Kenneth
Lay, encouraged Enron employees to buy stock in the company, calling it a "bargain." Sixty-seven days later, on December 2, Enron filed
for bankruptcy.

Even before the bankruptcy filing in November 2001, angry employees filed at least three lawsuits against Enron, complaining that

the company, as the sponsor of its 401(k) plan, had violated its obligations to look out for the employees. They claimed that the company executives had promoted Enron stock as a good investment for retirement savings when they must have known that the company was in trouble and the stock was overvalued.

Later, in January 2002, other Enron employees filed another lawsuit (Severed Enron Employees v. Northern Trust Company, class-action complaint, filed January 6, 2002), complaining, among other things, that Enron did not have an objective process for monitoring whether Enron stock made sense as an investment alternative in the 401(k) plan. The lawsuit also criticized Enron management for structuring its "financial dealings in such a complicated and impenetrable manner" that employees couldn't possibly evaluate the company's finances.

In February 2002, yet another employee lawsuit claimed that Enron had abused its 401(k) plan by encouraging employees to invest in Enron stock so that a large block of stock owned by employees would help fend off any hostile takeover of Enron. These employees said that Enron had perverted the purpose of the 401(k) plan by using it for the job security of the top Enron executives instead of for the financial security of rank-and-file Enron employees.

These lawsuits were still pending as this book went to press, but a review of other 401(k)-related lawsuits shows that employers' misuse and mishandling of their 401(k) plans, although not rampant, had occurred from time to time before the Enron collapse.

Beginning of a trend

In one case, employees of First Union Bank complained that First Union offered only its own mutual funds as investment alternatives in the First Union 401(k) plan. They said that First Union was "self-dealing" and was charging the plan participants excessive fees. First Union settled the case for $26 million and appointed an independent consultant to advise First Union in the future.

A recent 401(k) plan anti-fraud campaign by the U.S. Department of Labor (DOL) uncovered a small number of employers that had abused employee contributions by either using the money for corporate purposes or holding on to the money too long. The DOL requires that employees' paycheck deductions for contribution to their 401(k) accounts be placed in the 401(k) plan within 45 days, at the latest.

However, in one case, an employer and one of its officers had failed to deposit employees' payroll contributions into their 401(k) accounts within the time periods that the DOL requires. The employer and officer were required to pay $102,000, which represented interest on the late deposit amounts, based on the highest rate of return of any investment under the plan.

In another case, a paper box manufacturer failed to deposit more than two years' worth of employees' 401(k) contributions with the 401(k) plan service provider. By the time the company went out of business, more than $369,000 in 401(k) money was missing. After a DOL lawsuit filed on behalf of the employees, the company's fiduciary insurance policy deposited the money with the 401(k) plan service provider. However, the service provider's first checks to the former employees bounced because of an administrative snafu.

Sometimes the problem is the employer's initial neglect of its responsibility to oversee its 401(k) plan and then failure to communicate emerging issues to employees. This may have been what happened to Unisys employees who invested their 401(k) money in guaranteed investment contracts (GICs) from Executive Life Insurance Company.

When Unisys selected Executive Life GICs as investments for its 401(k) plan, Executive Life was well known in the industry to be heavily invested in junk bonds. As Executive Life collapsed in 1991, a large portion of the GICs in Unisys 401(k) accounts became worthless.

Unisys employees brought a class action lawsuit against Unisys for investing 401(k) plan assets in Executive Life GICs and for misleading the employees about Executive Life's financial condition. How the case was resolved may surprise you.

Executive Life and the Unisys 401(k)

In the fall of 1986, Burroughs Corporation and Sperry Corporation merged to form Unisys. Before the merger, both Sperry and Burroughs had maintained 401(k) plans for their employees. One of the funds in each of these plans invested in GICs, which are issued primarily by insurance companies.

Following the merger, the Burroughs and Sperry 401(k) plans were consolidated to form the Unisys 401(k) plan. The consolidation took effect in April 1988.

As did its predecessors, the Unisys 401(k) plan established an individual account for each participant and offered several investment alternatives for plan participants. There were six Unisys investment alternatives: the diversified fund, the indexed equity fund, the active equity fund, the Unisys common stock fund, the short-term investment fund, and the insurance contract fund. The insurance contract fund invested in GICs.

The old Sperry fixed income fund, also a vehicle for GICs, continued to exist, but it was closed to new contributions. As the GICs matured, the assets invested in the Sperry fixed income fund were reinvested in the new Unisys insurance contract fund. Assets in the old Burroughs guaranteed investment contract fund were likewise reinvested in that fund, unless a participant specified otherwise. Contributions to the Unisys insurance contract fund were allocated in proportion to the various GICs held in it.

The Unisys 401(k) plan allowed a participant to transfer assets from one equity fund to another once a month. Due to transfer limitation terms that were included in the contracts purchased for the GIC funds, however, asset transfers involving those funds were restricted. For example, all transfers between any of the GIC funds and the short-term investment fund, another low-risk, interest-earning vehicle, were absolutely prohibited.

Moreover, if assets were transferred from one of the GIC funds to the equity or Unisys common stock funds, a year had to pass before any assets could be transferred to the short-term investment fund. Similarly, if assets were transferred from the equity or the Unisys common stock funds to the short-term investment fund, the plan participant had to wait a year before he or she could transfer money out of one of the GIC Funds.

Unisys was its own 401(k) plan administrator. Its 401(k) administrative committee, established by the Unisys board of directors, carried out the provisions of the plans. The 401(k) investment committee, also established by the board, was responsible for the plan's investments.

The investment committee delegated day-to-day investment management responsibility for the GIC funds to two of the investment committee members and appointed outside service providers to manage investments in the plan's other funds. From time to time Unisys conducted a bid among insurance companies during which GIC contracts were selected for the appropriate GIC fund. These selections were subject to the approval of the investment committee.

Unisys did not have written guidelines for the bidding process or contract selection. The investment committee members did, however, have informal operating policies and procedures. In particular, they developed a rule that no more than 20 percent of GIC fund assets would be invested with any one insurance company.

After the merger in 1986, but before the 401(k) consolidation effective date in April 1988, two bids for the old Sperry fixed income fund were held. The first bid was conducted in June 1987 by an independent consultant that Sperry had used to assist in GIC selections. Before the bid day, the consulting firm mailed bid specifications on Unisys' behalf to a number of insurers, including the

Executive Life Insurance Company of California, inviting them to make a GIC proposal.

It was the consulting firm's practice to solicit bids only from insurers with a superior AAA rating (as to claims-paying ability) from Standard & Poors Corporation. At the time, Standard & Poors had rated Executive Life as a AAA company. Likewise, A.M. Best Company, another rating agency, had assigned Executive Life its highest rating of A$^+$. According to the consulting firm, however, the A$^+$ from A.M. Best didn't mean much because A.M. Best was overly generous with its ratings.

On the day of the bid, Unisys and the consulting firm reviewed material that Executive Life had provided about its financial condition and interviewed Executive Life representatives about the company's outlook. The consulting firm noted that purchasing Executive Life GICs would be "controversial" because of the junk bonds that Executive Life held in its portfolio.

Standard & Poors viewed the risk of Executive Life's junk bond investments as offset by other conservative aspects of the company's investment strategy. The consulting firm warned, however, that the Standard & Poors AAA rating was reliable only as long as Executive Life's junk bond holdings did not exceed 35 percent of its bond portfolio.

Ultimately, the consulting firm recommended that Unisys consider the purchase of a three-year GIC from Executive Life. Although Unisys accepted the consulting firm's advice to invest with Executive Life, it rejected the consulting firm's recommendation as to how long the contract should last. In order to get the highest interest rate that Executive Life offered—9.45 percent—Unisys purchased a five-year Executive Life GIC for approximately $30 million. Unisys also accepted GIC bids from Travelers Insurance Company and Seattle First Bank.

After the June 1987 bid, Unisys ended its contract with the consulting firm and did not hire a replacement. Unisys management believed that its personnel could select appropriate GICs without a consultant's help.

A second competitive GIC bid for the Sperry fixed income fund took place in December 1987. Relying heavily on Executive Life's ratings, which had not changed since June 1987, Unisys invested just more than $135 million in another five-year Executive Life GIC—this one paying 9.75 percent interest. Unisys purchased GICs from Seafirst Bank and Travelers Insurance Company as well, bearing interest rates of 9.25 percent and 9.15 percent, respectively.

Later, in January 1988, Unisys sponsored a GIC bid for its insurance contract fund. Once again, based on the high marks Executive Life continued to receive from the rating agencies, Unisys invested about $46 million in a third five-year, 9.48 percent interest-paying Executive Life GIC, bringing the total investment in GICs issued by Executive Life to $213 million.

All during this time, communications to Unisys 401(k) plan participants described the GIC funds as designed to preserve capital and accumulate interest. These communications consistently emphasized that investments in GICs were "guaranteed" by the issuing insurance companies.

Burroughs 401(k) communication materials (for its GIC funds that were closed to new investments) stated that the goal of the guaranteed insurance contract fund was "to preserve the amount invested and to guarantee a rate of return," and that "[i]n addition to the interest earned, the insurance company guarantees the principal of the fund. [Y]our account cannot go down in value; it will always be worth as much as you put in plus your share of the interest earned under the contract." Similarly, the Sperry fixed income fund materials declared that "each year's minimum [interest] rate is guaranteed for an entire year."

Likewise, some prospectuses distributed in the spring of 1988 to Unisys 401(k) plan participants stated that the Unisys insurance contract fund was intended "to preserve capital while earning interest income." The prospectuses described the fund as "invested in contracts with insurance companies and other financial institutions which guarantee repayment of principal with interest at a fixed or fixed minimum rate for specified periods...."

However, one Unisys 401(k) prospectus noted that "[Unisys] does not guarantee the repayment of principal or interest." Although earlier prospectuses did not include this warning, it was subsequently included in a 1988 supplement to each. Additionally, the prospectuses pointed out that assets of the insurance contract fund were invested in contracts issued by Executive Life.

According to the decision in Meinhardt v. Unisys (issued on January 5, 1996), the 1988 summary plan descriptions (SPDs) for the various 401(k) plans provided that the investment objective of the insurance contract fund was to "[p]reserve the amount invested while earning interest income." The SPDs described the funds' investment strategy as "[t]ypically contracts of between 3 and 7 years with various insurance companies and other financial institutions which guarantee the principal and a specified rate of return for the life of each contract," and explained that the future performance of any of the funds was not certain:

> [b]enefits available are based on your savings plan value at the time of distribution. Your payments from the Plan are subject to the performance of the funds in which your accounts are invested. If the value declines, you may receive less from the Plan than you and the Company contributed.

The 1988 and 1990 prospectuses for the 401(k) plans pointed out:

> [T]he Plan is subject to some, but not all, of the provisions of [ERISA]...which [a]mong other things...set minimum standards of fiduciary responsibility, establish minimum standards for participation and vesting, and require that each member be furnished with an annual report of financial

condition and a comprehensive description of the member's rights under the Plan.

The SPDs of the 401(k) plans informed the participants:

[Y]ou are entitled to certain rights and protections under [ERISA]....In addition to creating rights for Plan participants, ERISA imposes duties upon the people who are responsible for the operation of employee benefit plans. The people who operate the [Unisys 401(k) Plan], called 'fiduciaries' of the Plans, have a duty to [operate] prudently, in your interest and that of all members and beneficiaries.

After the prospectuses and the SPDs were distributed, the investment committee received correspondence in 1988 and 1989 from individual participants, including Henry Zylla, the president of one of Unisys's local unions. Zylla questioned whether Executive Life GICs should have been purchased, given the insurer's high-risk investments. In response to Zylla, Unisys wrote that the investment committee did not invite "risky" companies to its GIC bids, that its GIC selection process continuously emphasized "safety," and that all of the contracts it selected for the GIC Funds carried investment-grade credit ratings.

In January 1990, some two years after Unisys's last Executive Life GIC purchase, Executive Life announced that it had written down $515 million in assets due to losses in its bond portfolio. After this announcement, Executive Life's credit ratings were lowered from AAA to A by Standard & Poors, from A$^+$ to A by A.M. Best, and from A1 to BAA2 by a third rating company, Moody's Investors Service.

Concerned that a flood of policy and other contract surrenders would cause a liquidity crisis that it would be unable to overcome, Executive Life began meeting with its investors to discuss its financial condition. When representatives of Executive Life and Unisys met in

January 1990, Executive Life assured Unisys that it would continue to meet its obligations and survive the current crisis.

In February 1990, members of the investment committee and other Unisys personnel met to discuss the questions that Unisys had received from plan participants about Executive Life. After some debate, Unisys said that it would send an updated prospectus with a cover letter to all plan participants about Executive Life's financial condition.

In late March 1990, Unisys sent a revised prospectus to each participant. The prospectus stated that "an investment in any of the investment funds involves some degree of risk." It also said that many factors, including the "financial stability of the institutions in which assets are invested, the quality of the investment portfolios of those institutions, and other economic developments will affect...the value of a [participant's] investment in those funds." In bold letters, the prospectus added that "[a]s a result, there is no assurance that at any point in time the value of an investment in any fund will not be lower than the original amount invested."

As for the Unisys insurance contract fund, the revised prospectus stated that its "objective...is to preserve capital while earning interest income" and characterized its investments as "contractual obligation[s]" of the issuer (the insurance company). It pointed out that the "repayment of principal and interest is necessarily subject to the [issuer's] ability to pay...[such that] a downturn or loss in one or more areas of the [issuer's] investment portfolio could have an adverse effect on the stability of the [issuer]."

As an earlier prospectus did, the revised prospectus stated that "[Unisys] does not guarantee the repayment of principal or interest." It also informed participants that the investment committee's guidelines required that Unisys purchase GICs from insurers rated "Secure" by Standard & Poor's, "Highest Investment Quality" by Moody's Investors Service, or "Superior" or "Excellent" by A.M. Best, but that "[c]ontracts issued by an insurance company or other institution whose rating is downgraded subsequent to selection may continue to be held in the fund." Finally, it identified Executive Life as one of the companies from which GICs had been purchased.

With the prospectus, participants received a cover letter from a vice president of Unisys human resources, encouraging participants to review the prospectus carefully and reminding them that Unisys would not give advice as to appropriate investment strategy. The cover letter discussed the "troubled 'junk bond' market and the effect, if any, that such problems would have on the [GIC Funds]." It pointed out that the repayment of principal and interest under GICs necessarily and entirely depended on the ability of the insurer to meet its obligations.

In addition, the letter said that Unisys did not guarantee the GICs. The financial stability of an insurer depended on the success of its own portfolio. An insurers' investment in junk bonds could have an adverse effect on the insurer's financial stability. Lastly, the letter stated that only those institutions with a "secure" credit rating at the time of a contract bid would be selected for investment.

Although an early draft of this letter specifically mentioned Executive Life, the letter the participants eventually received did not. The early draft's reference to Executive Life's $515 million asset writedown was removed. A statement disclosing the magnitude of the proportion of fixed income and insurance contract fund investments in Executive Life was crossed out because it "could cause panic." And a statement about informative news articles was deleted because it "could cause more concern." A comment on the draft stated: "The overall content and tone do [not] sooth[e] any fears and may in fact stir more interest in this subject than it deserves." (The quoted material in this section comes from the decision in Meinhardt v. Unisys, issued on January 5, 1996.)

This letter to the Unisys 401(k) plan participants was accompanied by an enclosure that listed all of the GICs held in the GIC funds at that time, with investment value, maturity dates, and the bid day and current ratings of the issuing insurer. The enclosure revealed that Executive Life GICs had a combined book value of more than $200 million, maturity dates of June 1991, June and September 1992, and March, June, and August 1993. It also showed the recent decline in ratings that Executive Life had suffered. The revised prospectus, cover letter, and enclosure were the only communications Unisys made to all participants after Executive Life announced its $515 million asset write-down.

At about the same time, Unisys distributed to its human resources personnel a copy of a letter from Executive Life that portrayed the company as "healthy," "financially strong," and "capable of providing all the benefits promised." The letter included written responses to specific questions about Executive Life that individual participants might ask. For example, individuals who asked the Unisys human re-sources department, "How many people ever lost their money in this kind of thing?" were to be told, "I don't remember one time they even halfway defaulted."

In March 1990, Unisys also met with union employees and re-sponded to participants' inquiries about Executive Life's financial sta-tus. Unisys did not, however, disclose two other decisions it had made: one involving its chairman's retirement annuity and the second, an investment committee resolution.

A few months after sending the revised prospectus to participants, Unisys decided to replace a $500,000 retirement annuity issued by Executive Life for Unisys's chairman with an annuity from another insurer—at some expense to Unisys. The second decision was made at an investment committee meeting in August 1990. The committee decided "that in the event of a default in any of the guaranteed in-vestment contracts...distribution to plan participants will be reduced by that portion of the participant's account held in the defaulted contract."

Seeking to reduce the waiting period for asset transfers between "noncompeting" funds and the GIC Funds from 12 months to six, Unisys contacted the issuers from whom GICs had been purchased and asked that they agree to appropriate contract modifications. In exchange for Executive Life's consent to a waiting period reduction in the contracts it had issued to the 401(k) plan, Unisys executed a letter agreement in October 1990, which provided in part:

> Unisys Corporation hereby further agrees that neither it nor its affiliates, employees, agents or other representatives will communicate with Plan participants regarding the financial condition or prospects of Executive Life nor issue any other communication regarding Executive Life which could be reasonably viewed as attempting to influence the investment choices of Plan participants without first obtaining Executive Life's written approval of such communication. In the event such prior written approval is not obtained, Executive Life may elect to not honor employee requests for withdrawals or reallocations provided that Executive Life reasonably believes that such requests were the direct result of such communication.

During this time, Executive Life's financial condition was widely reported in the financial press. Eventually, in April 1991, the California Commissioner of Insurance seized Executive Life, placed it in conservatorship, and issued a moratorium on all payments from the insurer. As a result, Unisys isolated and froze the balance in any participant account invested in Executive Life by way of the fixed income and/or insurance contract funds. At this time, 30 percent of the fixed income fund and 7 percent of the insurance contract fund were invested with Executive Life. In December 1991, the Superior Court of California declared Executive Life insolvent.

The employees' class action lawsuit bounced back and forth between a federal trial court and a federal appellate court. In the end, the courts decided that Unisys had not breached its duties to the 401(k) plan participants. The case was sent to the United States Supreme Court, but it declined to review it.

Enron's legal legacy

Since Enron's collapse, at least 115 lawsuits have been filed against 35 employers with complaints about the mishandling of 401(k) plans. At least 22 of the defendants are big companies, such as WorldCom, Qwest, and Global Crossing. In January 2003, Rite Aid settled its 401(k) lawsuit for $9.5 million.

Observers say that the U.S. Department of Labor's stance in the Enron lawsuits is encouraging the current wave of 401(k) litigation. Although not a party to the lawsuit, the DOL submitted a 61-page brief to the court that is handling one of the Enron 401(k) cases.

The DOL's brief supports the claims that top Enron executives are legally responsible for the 401(k) plan's losses in Enron stock. The brief states, "ERISA's fiduciary obligations…do not permit fiduciaries to ignore grave risks to plan assets, stand idly by while participants' retirement security is destroyed, and then blithely assert that they had no responsibility for the resulting harm."

Many lawyers view this legal brief as clarifying the existing law governing 401(k) plan sponsors. The outcomes of the Enron 401(k) lawsuits are expected to influence the shape of 401(k) owners' legal rights in the future.

The Enron 401(k) fiasco is already influencing how troubled companies are handling employer stock in their 401(k) plans. Shortly before United Airlines filed for bankruptcy in December 2002, United's 401(k) plan sold all of United stock in the plan—without asking the plan participants.

Can you rely on your 401(k) plan's administrators to catch problems early? Maybe not. Certainly you can't expect the federal government to keep a sharp eye on every 401(k) plan in the country. You may have to be your own 401(k) watchdog.

If you see signs that your 401(k) plan may be in trouble, ask your plan's service provider and your company's human resources department for an explanation. If you're not satisfied with the explanation, call the Department of Labor at 1-202-219-8211.

Don't be shy about checking up on the management of your 401(k) plan. Mismanagement could mean the loss of some or all of your retirement savings.

Signs That Your 401(k) Plan
May Be in Trouble

- Your account balance appears inaccurate.

- Your employer fails to deposit your contribution to the plan on time.

- Investments listed on your statement are not what you authorized.

- Your employer has recently experienced severe financial difficulty.

- Your 401(k) account statement is consistently late or comes at irregular intervals.

- A significant drop in your account balance cannot be explained by normal market volatility.

- Your 401(k) account statement shows that your contribution from your paycheck was not made.

- Former employees are having trouble getting their benefits paid on time or in the correct amounts.

- The press reports that the financial institution that runs one or more of your 401(k) plan's investment alternatives is having financial problems.

- There are frequent and unexplained changes in investment managers or consultants.

Chapter 5

Avoiding Excessive
401(k) Fees

"Money is a guarantee that we may have what we want in the future. Though we need nothing at the moment it insures the possibility of satisfying a new desire when it arises."

—Aristotle

FEES AND EXPENSES LOWER YOUR 401(K) account's investment returns, and your retirement income. Although contributions to your account and the earnings on your investments increase your retirement income, 401(k) fees may reduce the value of your account significantly.

> **Example.** Sam is an employee with 35 years until retirement and a current 401(k) account balance of $25,000. If the rate of return on the investments in his account over the next 35 years averages 7 percent and fees and expenses reduce his average returns by 0.5 percent, his account balance will grow to $227,000 at retirement, even if Sam contributes nothing else to his account. However, if fees and expenses are 1.5 percent, Sam's account balance will grow to only $163,000. The 1-percent difference in fees and expenses would reduce Sam's account balance at retirement by 28 percent.

As a 401(k) account owner, you may like the chance to build re-tirement savings, but you may not realize what it costs you. Fees can take away as much as 3 percent of your 401(k) account balance every year. As the previous example shows, the long-term effect of these fees on your retirement savings can be significant. Fortunately, many of these fees are within your control.

First, a few words about service providers and employers

There are many ways 401(k) plan investments and services are provided and paid for. Your employer may be paying for some of the services. It may also negotiate for, on your behalf, the fees that you pay for various services and investment alternatives in your 401(k) plan.

Each 401(k) service provider (that is, investment manager, trustee, record-keeper, and communications firm) may be charging separate fees. This is sometimes called an unbundled arrangement.

However, one service provider may be providing all of the various services and investment alternatives for one fee structure. This is some-times called a bundled arrangement.

Some 401(k) plans use an arrangement that combines a single pro-vider for administrative services with a number of other providers for investment alternatives. The fees to all of these service providers should be considered to figure out the cost of running a 401(k) plan.

If this sounds complicated, that's because it is. Even some em-ployee benefits experts have trouble figuring out 401(k) fees.

In recent years, the number of investment alternatives typically offered under 401(k) plans has increased dramatically. The level and types of services provided to participants have increased as well.

These changes may give today's employees who direct their 401(k) investments greater opportunity than ever to manage their retirement savings. However, the changes have made 401(k) plans more expen-sive than ever before. More employers are passing on these costs to plan participants.

Note: A recent survey of 401(k) plans (each with about 200 participants and an average of $8 million in assets) found that total fees and expenses averaged $526 per participant annually.

By law, your employer must consider the fees and expenses that your plan pays. The Employee Retirement Income Security Act of 1974 (ERISA) requires your employer to follow certain rules in managing its 401(k) plan. As a 401(k) plan sponsor, your employer has a fiduciary responsibility. It is held to high standards and must act solely in the interest of the plan participants and their beneficiaries. Among other things, this means that your employer must:

- Establish an appropriate process for selecting investment alternatives and service providers.

- Ensure that fees that are paid to service providers and other expenses of the plan are reasonable.

- Select investment alternatives that are appropriate and adequately diversified.

- Monitor investment alternatives and service providers to see that they continue to be appropriate choices.

Now, about those fees

To understand how fees affect your retirement savings, you should know about the different types of fees and expenses and the different ways in which they are charged. Your 401(k) plan's fees and expenses generally fall into three categories: investment fees, individual service fees, and plan administration fees.

Investment fees are the largest component of 401(k) plan fees and expenses. These fees are charged as a percentage of the money in your 401(k) account. You should pay close attention to these fees, because service providers deduct them directly from your investment returns. Your net total return is your return after these fees have been deducted. These fees are not specifically identified on your 401(k) account statements.

Your 401(k) service provider may charge many types of fees for your use of various investment alternatives. These fees, which can be referred to by different terms, include sales charges, which are also known as loads or commissions. These are basically transaction costs for the buying and selling of shares. They may be computed in different ways, depending upon the particular investment alternative.

> *Note: If you transfer money frequently from one investment alternative to another, you may be paying substantial charges and other fees that you don't even know about.*

Management fees (also known as investment advisory fees or account maintenance fees) are ongoing charges for managing the assets of the investment fund. They are generally stated as a percentage of the amount of assets invested in the fund. Sometimes management fees may be used to cover administrative expenses.

Management fees can vary widely, depending on the service provider and the investment alternatives. Investments that require significant management, research, and monitoring services generally will have higher fees.

> *Note: Stock funds tend to charge higher fees than bond funds. Index funds tend to charge the lowest fees of all.*

Other fees cover services (such as record-keeping, furnishing statements, toll-free telephone numbers, and investment advice) involved in the day-to-day management of investment products. They may be stated either as a flat fee or as a percentage of the amount of assets invested in the fund.

Most investments offered under 401(k) plans today pool the money of a large number of individual investors. Pooling money makes it possible for individual participants to diversify investments, to benefit from economies of scale, and to lower their transaction costs. These funds may invest in stocks, bonds, real estate, and other investments.

Larger plans are more likely to pool investments on their own—for example, by using a separate account held with a financial institution. Smaller plans generally invest in pooled investments offered by financial institutions, such as banks, insurance companies, or mutual funds. Generally, the participant pays investment-related fees, usually charged as a percentage of assets invested.

> *Note: Smaller 401(k) plans tend to have higher fees—sometimes much higher—than large plans.*

Some fees are unique to specific types of investments. Here are brief descriptions of some of the more common investment alternatives that 401(k) plans offer and explanations of some of the different terms or unique fees associated with them.

Mutual funds

Mutual funds pool and invest the money of many individuals. Shares in a mutual fund represent a part of the mutual fund's holdings. An investment professional manages the portfolio of securities held by a mutual fund following a specific investment policy.

According to a March 2003 report by the U.S. General Accounting Office, the fees charged by large stock mutual funds increased from an average 0.63 percent of assets in 1999 to an average 0.70 percent of assets in 2001. The drop in assets held by many stock funds since 1999 may have caused the rise in expense ratios because the same management expenses are being spread out over a smaller base.

In addition to investment management and administration fees, you may find that some mutual funds assess sales charges (discussed in the previous section). These charges may be paid when you invest in a fund (known as a front-end load) or when you sell shares (known as a back-end load, deferred sales charge, or redemption fee).

A front-end load is deducted up front and, therefore, reduces the amount of your initial investment. A back-end load is determined by how long you keep your investment. There are various types of back-end loads, including some that decrease and eventually disappear over time. A back-end load is paid when the shares are sold. So, if you decide to sell a fund share when a back-end load is in effect, you will be charged the fee.

Mutual funds may also charge "Rule 12b-1 fees," which are on-going fees paid out of fund assets. Rule 12b-1 fees may be used to pay commissions to brokers and other salespersons, to pay for advertising and other costs of promoting the fund to investors, and to pay various service providers to a 401(k) plan according to a bundled services arrangement. They are usually between 0.25 percent and 1 percent of assets annually.

Some mutual funds may be advertised as no-load funds. This can mean that there is no front- or back-end load. However, there may be a Rule 12b-1 fee.

Funds that are "actively managed" have an investment advisor who continually researches, monitors, and actively trades the holdings of the fund to seek a higher return than average market returns. Funds with active management generally have higher fees.

The higher fees are associated with the more active management provided and sales charges from the higher level of trading activity. Although actively managed funds seek to provide higher returns than the market, neither active management nor higher fees necessarily guarantee higher returns.

Note: Actively managed mutual funds typically do not perform better than passively managed index funds.

Funds that are "passively managed" generally have lower management fees. Passively managed funds try to get the investment results of an established market index, such as the Standard & Poor's

500, by duplicating the holdings included in the index. Thus, passively managed funds require little research or trading activity.

Some other 401(k) investments

A collective investment fund is a trust fund managed by a bank or trust company that pools investments of 401(k) plans and other similar investors. Each investor has a proportionate interest in the trust fund assets. For example, if a collective investment fund holds $10 million in assets and your investment in the fund is $10,000, you have a 0.1-percent interest in the fund.

Different collective investment funds may have different investment objectives. There are no front- or back-end fees associated with a collective investment fund, but there are investment management and administrative fees.

Insurance companies frequently offer a range of investment alternatives for 401(k) plans through a group variable annuity contract between an insurance company and an employer on behalf of a plan. The variable annuity contract "wraps" around investment alternatives, often a number of mutual funds. Participants select from among the investment alternatives offered, and the returns to their individual accounts vary with their choice of investments.

Variable annuities also include one or more insurance elements, which are not present in other investment alternatives. Generally, these elements include an annuity feature, interest and expense guarantees, and any death benefit provided during the term of the contract. In addition to investment management fees and administration fees, you may find insurance-related charges are associated with investment alternatives that include an insurance component. They include items such as sales expenses, mortality risk charges, and the cost of issuing and administering contracts.

You may also find surrender and transfer charges, which are fees an insurance company may charge when an employer terminates a contract (in other words, withdraws the plan's investment) before the term of the contract expires or if you withdraw an amount from the contract. This fee may be imposed if these events occur before the expiration of a stated period. The fee normally decreases over time. It is similar to an early withdrawal penalty on a bank certificate of deposit or to a back-end load or redemption fee charged by some mutual funds.

A common fixed income investment alternative, a pooled GIC fund generally includes a number of contracts issued by an insurance company or bank paying an interest rate that blends the fixed interest rates of each of the GICs included in the pool. Investment management and administrative fees are associated with the pooled GIC fund.

Service and administration fees

Individual service fees are charged according to your 401(k) plan's optional features. They are charged separately to your 401(k) account if you choose to take advantage of a particular plan feature. For example, individual service fees may be charged to a participant who takes a loan from the plan or who executes participant investment directions.

Plan administration fees pay for the day-to-day operations of a 401(k) plan including plan record keeping, accounting, legal, and trustee services. Today a 401(k) plan also may offer a host of additional services, such as telephone voice response systems, access to a customer service representative, educational seminars, retirement planning software, investment advice, electronic access to plan information, daily valuation, and online transactions.

Sometimes, fees are deducted directly from your 401(k) investment returns to cover the costs of administrative services. Other times, your employer pays for these administrative costs.

> *Note: Unless your employer covers the entire administrative cost of your 401(k) plan, you may be paying for a share of your plan's education products and services and even for customer service.*

When your 401(k) plan pays for them, administrative fees are either allocated among individual 401(k) accounts according to account balance (so that participants with larger account balances pay more of the allocated expenses) or charged as a flat fee against each participant's account. Either way, the more services from your 401(k) service provider, the higher the fees it charges.

What is being charged to your 401(k) account?

Your 401(k) plan administrator should provide you, upon your request, with certain documents that help you evaluate your plan's fees and expenses. For example, you can ask for a prospectus for each of your plan's investment alternatives to find out about any transaction fees and expenses that will be charged against your account balance for that investment alternative.

Your account statement shows the total assets in your account, how they are invested, and any increases (or decreases) in your investments during the period covered by the statement. It may—or may not—also show administrative expenses charged to your account. Account statements are provided once a year upon request, unless your plan document provides otherwise.

Your 401(k) plan's summary plan description (SPD) will tell you what the plan provides and how it operates. It may tell you if administrative expenses are paid by your plan, rather than by your employer, and how those expenses are allocated among plan participants. A copy of the SPD is furnished to participants when they join a plan and every five years if there are major changes or every 10 years if there is no modification.

Your 401(k) plan's Form 5500 (annual report) contains information regarding the plan's assets, liabilities, income, and expenses and shows the aggregate administrative fees and other expenses paid by the plan. However, it will not show expenses deducted from investment results or fees and expenses paid by individual accounts. Fees that your employer paid also will not be shown.

You may examine your plan's Form 5500 for free. If you request a copy of your plan's Form 5500 from the plan administrator, there may be a copying charge. In general, a summary annual report is distributed to you each year.

> *Note: Some employers pay almost nothing to make a 401(k) plan available to their employees. The result is that all of the 401(k) fees are taken from the participants' accounts.*

The National Association of Securities Dealers (NASD) has a free online calculator at *www.nasdr.com/fundcalc* that shows the long-term effect of fees and expenses. If, after you do your own analysis, you have questions regarding the rates of return or fees of your plan's investment alternatives, ask your plan administrator to explain.

If the services and investment alternatives under your plan are offered through a bundled program, then some or all of the costs of plan services may not be separately charged to the plan or to your employer. For example, the asset-based fees charged on investments possibly may subsidize these costs. Compare the services received in light of the total fees paid.

Plans with more total assets may be able to lower fees by using special funds or classes of stock in funds, which generally are sold to larger group investors. Retail or brand name funds, which are also marketed to individual and small group investors, tend to be listed in the daily newspaper and typically charge higher fees.

Optional features, such as participant loan programs and insurance benefits offered under variable annuity contracts, involve additional costs. Chances are, the cost of using these programs is passed along to you. Consider whether the benefit of such features is worth the cost.

401(k) Fees Checklist

- What are the investment alternatives that your company's 401(k) plan offers?

- Do you have all available documentation about the investment alternatives under your plan and the fees charged to your plan?

- What types of investment education are available under your plan?

- What arrangement is used to provide services under your plan? Does a single provider provide any or all of the services or investment alternatives?

- Do you and other participants use most or all of the optional services offered under your 401(k) plan, such as participant loan programs and insurance coverage?

- If administrative services are paid separately from investment management fees, are they paid for by the plan, paid for by your employer, or are they shared?

- Do any of the investment alternatives track an established market index, or is a higher level of investment management services provided for all investment alternatives?

- Do any of the investment alternatives under your plan include sales charges (such as loads or commissions)?

- Do any of the investment alternatives under your plan include any fees related to specific investments, such as Rule 12b-1 fees, insurance charges or surrender fees, and what do they cover?

Chapter 6

Taking Out Your Money Wisely

"A rolling stone gathers no moss."

—Plublius Syrus, circa 42 B.C.

THIS CHAPTER MUST BEGIN WITH A confession from the author. When she was 24 years old, she left her three-year career with General Electric Company to travel around the world on a shoestring. Her shoestring was $10,000 saved up in her General Electric 401(k) account. She took the 401(k) distribution, did not roll it over, and paid the 10-percent early-withdrawal penalty. However, by timing her departure for early February and earning no other income for the rest of that year, she paid minimal income tax on the distribution.

Was handling the 401(k) distribution in this manner a wise choice? Only if wise choices are not limited to those that protect long-term financial security. If your goal when you leave your employer is financial security for retirement, do the rollover.

More specifically, consider making it a direct rollover to a traditional individual retirement account (IRA). And try to avoid administrative delays in making the transfer. Later, consider converting the traditional IRA to a Roth IRA, if possible.

When you leave your employer—whether at retirement or earlier— you may withdraw cash or other assets from your 401(k) account in an eligible rollover distribution. Two ways to use your pre-tax 401(k) money without leaving your employer are in case of hardship or with a 401(k) loan.

401(k) rollovers

If you have an eligible rollover distribution, you may postpone the tax on the distribution and avoid the 10-percent penalty that may apply by rolling the distribution over to another qualified plan or a traditional IRA. An eligible rollover distribution is any distribution from your 401(k) account except:

- ◆ Hardship distributions (discussed later in this chapter).
- ◆ The cost of life insurance coverage.
- ◆ A required minimum distribution (discussed in Chapter 7).
- ◆ Corrective distributions of excess contributions or excess deferrals.
- ◆ A 401(k) loan (discussed later in this chapter) that is treated as a distribution because it does not satisfy certain requirements.
- ◆ Any of a series of substantially equal periodic payments.

In addition, a distribution to your beneficiary generally is not treated as an eligible rollover distribution. However, see the discussion of qualified domestic relations orders (QDROs) later in this chapter. Also, see the discussion of rollovers by a surviving spouse on page 106.

You may be able to roll over the nontaxable part of a distribution (such as any after-tax contributions) made to another qualified plan or a traditional IRA. The transfer must be made either through a direct rollover to a qualified plan that separately accounts for the taxable and nontaxable parts of the rollover or through a rollover to a traditional IRA.

You can choose to have any part or all of an eligible rollover distribution paid directly to another 401(k) plan that accepts rollover distributions or to a traditional IRA. If you choose the direct rollover alternative, no tax will be withheld from any part of the distribution that is directly paid to the trustee of the other plan. If any part of the eligible rollover distribution is paid to you, the payer must generally withhold 20 percent of it for income tax.

However, the full amount is treated as distributed to you even though you actually receive only 80 percent. You generally must include in income any part (including the part withheld) that you do not roll over within 60 days to another 401(k) plan or to a traditional IRA.

Tax-withholding requirements

When you receive an eligible rollover distribution, your former employer must withhold 20 percent of it for federal income taxes. This rule applies even if you plan to roll over the distribution to another 401(k) plan or to an IRA.

Again, you can avoid withholding by choosing the direct rollover alternative. However, the appreciated portion of employer stock that is distributed to you is not subject to withholding. (See Appendix B.)

The tax law favors direct rollovers of 401(k) money over premature cash distributions to the 401(k) account owner. If you decide to take a cash distribution be prepared for the consequences, which are outlined in Figure 6-1.

	Figure 6-1. Tax Consequences: 401(k) Distribution to You vs. Direct Rollover	
Affected item	**Result of a distribution to you**	**Result of a direct rollover**
Withholding	The payer must withhold 20 percent of the taxable part.	There is no withholding.
10-percent penalty	If you are younger than 59½, a 10-percent penalty may apply to the taxable part (including an amount equal to the tax withheld) that is not rolled over.	There is no 10-percent penalty.
When to report as income	Any taxable part (including the taxable part of any amount withheld) not rolled over is income to you in the year paid.	Any taxable part is not income to you until later distributed to you from the new plan or IRA.

If the part of the distribution you want to roll over exceeds the amount you actually received (because of tax withholding), you will have to get money from some other source (such as your savings or borrowed amounts) to add to the amount you actually received.

> **Example.** You receive an eligible rollover distribution of $10,000 from your 401(k) plan. Your employer withholds $2,000, so you actually receive only $8,000. If you want to roll over the entire $10,000 to postpone paying taxes, you will have to get $2,000 from some other source to add to the $8,000 you actually received. If you roll over only $8,000, you must include the $2,000 not rolled over in your income for the distribution year. Also, you may be subject to the 10-percent penalty on the $2,000 if it was distributed to you before you reached age 59½.

You generally must complete the rollover of an eligible rollover distribution paid to you by the 60th day following the day on which you receive the distribution from your employer's plan. The IRS may waive the 60-day requirement for a good reason, such as a casualty, disaster, or other event beyond your reasonable control.

> **Example.** In the previous example, you received the distribution on June 30, 2003. To postpone paying taxes, you must complete the rollover by August 29, 2003, the 60th day following June 30.

The 10-percent penalty and its exceptions

If you are younger than 59½ when a distribution is paid to you, you may have to pay a 10-percent penalty (in addition to the regular income tax) on the taxable part (including any tax withheld) that you do not roll over. The penalty does not apply to distributions that are:

- Made as part of a series of "substantially equal periodic payments."

- Made because you are totally and permanently disabled.

- Made to your beneficiaries after your death.

- Made after you leave your employer in or after the year you reached age 55.

- Paid to an alternate payee (such as a former spouse) under a qualified domestic relations order (QDRO).

- Used to pay deductible medical expenses that exceed 7.5 percent of your adjusted gross income (whether or not you itemize your deductions for the year).

- Due to an IRS levy of your 401(k) account.

Rollovers of non-cash assets

To roll over an eligible rollover distribution of noncash assets, such as mutual funds, you must either roll over the actual property distributed or sell it and roll over the proceeds. You may not keep the distributed property and roll over cash or other property.

If you sell the distributed property and roll over all the proceeds, no gain or loss is recognized on the sale. The sale proceeds (including any portion that represents appreciation) are treated as part of the distribution and are not included in your gross income for tax purposes.

If you roll over only part of the proceeds, you are taxed on the part that you keep. You must allocate the proceeds you keep between the part that represents ordinary income from the distribution (its value upon distribution) and the part that represents gain or loss from the sale (its change in value from its distribution to its sale).

> **Example 1.** On September 6, 2003, Frank received an eligible rollover distribution from his 401(k) plan of $50,000 in nonemployer stock. On September 27, 2003, he sold the stock for $60,000. On October 4, 2003, he contributed $60,000 cash to a traditional IRA. Frank does not include either the $50,000 eligible rollover distribution or the $10,000 gain from the sale of the stock in his income that year. The entire $60,000 rolled over will be ordinary income when he withdraws it from his IRA.

> **Example 2.** The facts are the same as in Example 1, except that Frank sold the stock for $40,000 and contributed $40,000 to the IRA. Frank does not include the $50,000 eligible rollover distribution in his income and does not deduct the $10,000 loss from the sale of the stock. The $40,000 rolled over will be ordinary income when he withdraws it from his IRA.

Example 3. The facts are the same as in Example 1, except that Frank rolled over only $45,000 of the $60,000 proceeds from the sale of the stock. The $15,000 proceeds he did not roll over includes part of the gain from the stock sale. Frank reports $2,500 ($10,000/$60,000 × $15,000) as capital gain and $12,500 ($50,000/$60,000 × $15,000) as ordinary income.

Example 4. The facts are the same as in Example 2, except that Frank rolled over only $25,000 of the $40,000 proceeds from the sale of the stock. The $15,000 proceeds he did not roll over includes part of the loss from the stock sale. Frank reports $3,750 ($10,000/$40,000 × $15,000) capital loss and $18,750 ($50,000/$40,000 × $15,000) ordinary income.

Other employer plan vs. a traditional IRA

Here are at least five reasons why a rollover to a traditional IRA may be better than a rollover to a qualified plan with another employer:

1. Generally, you would need to leave the new employer to access the funds under the most favorable terms.

2. The distribution rules of the IRA trustee to which you roll over the distribution, in terms of its restrictions and their tax consequences, may be better for you than the rules that apply to your new employer's plan.

3. The qualified plan may have a policy of distributing your entire account balance to your beneficiary when you die, which could have adverse tax consequences. (See Chapter 7.)

4. The traditional IRA may offer more investment choices.

5. The traditional IRAs may be subject to fewer administrative fees.

However, if you are thinking about declaring bankruptcy any time soon, consider keeping the money in your old 401(k) account, if possible, instead of rolling it over. (For more information, see the discussion about creditors later in this chapter and consult a bankruptcy attorney.)

Avoiding rollover delays

Many individuals transfer their 401(k) account balances to another qualified plan or traditional IRA without a hitch. If your transfer goes smoothly, count on the whole process taking two to three weeks.

However, this time frame may vary depending upon the assets, types of accounts, and institutions involved in the transfer. Transfers may be delayed if:

- ◆ The wrong transfer form is used.
- ◆ The transfer form has been incorrectly completed.
- ◆ The transfer involves a request to liquidate some or all of your assets.
- ◆ The transfer is from one type of account into a different type of account.
- ◆ A change in the ownership of the funds is involved.

Use the correct form to ensure that your transfer goes smoothly. Some financial institutions allow you to use one form for all account transfers; others have different forms depending on the type of account to which you are transferring (for example, an IRA account). To get the right form, call the new financial institution where you want to transfer your account or visit its Web site.

As you start filling in the transfer form, review the account statement from your old 401(k) plan service provider. Financial institutions generally require you to attach a copy of your most recent account statement to the transfer form.

The form usually asks for the name on your account, the type of account you want to transfer, account number, the financial institution where the account is held, and your Social Security number. Be sure you provide this information exactly as it appears on your old account statement.

For instance, if your middle name or initial appears on your old account statement, you may run into delays if you forget to include it. When transferring only some of the investments in your account, carefully list on the form the investments that you want to transfer.

If you are a surviving spouse or an alternate payee, you are also changing ownership at the time of the transfer. This may delay the transfer. You may need to provide the documents that prove a change in ownership, such as a marriage certificate and death certificate, or divorce decree and qualified domestic relations order.

If you have questions about how to complete the form, contact the new financial institution for help. Once completed, keep a copy of the form for your records. All transfers start and end with your new financial institution, but the old 401(k) plan needs to take action, too.

Sometimes, a transfer is made manually instead of electronically. This occurs when your 401(k) funds are with a mutual fund company that does not participate in the Automated Customer Account Transfer Service (ACATS). This also may occur if you want to liquidate assets other than the money market fund in your account.

There are no set time frames for completing a manual transfer with these financial institutions. For that reason—and the potential risk of market volatility should there be any delay—you may not want to liquidate any assets via instructions on the transfer form.

A manual transfer may also occur when you request a partial transfer from your 401(k) account to an IRA trustee. Financial institutions are required to complete these requests in a reasonable amount of time.

Some types of investments may not be transferred. These investments include:

- ◆ Annuities.

- ◆ Bankrupt securities.

- ◆ Investment alternatives offered exclusively by your old 401(k) plan.

- ◆ Mutual funds or money market funds not available for your IRA or in your new employer's 401(k) plan.

If your request includes some of these nontransferable investments, it may take longer to resolve your transfer. Your old 401(k) plan is required to transfer whatever investments it can through ACATS and ask you what you want to do with the others. You generally have two choices: either sell the nontransferable investment and transfer the cash, or leave the investment with your old 401(k) plan.

Be aware that your old 401(k) plan may charge you a fee for the transfer to cover administrative costs. Sometimes, the recipient of your 401(k) money will also charge a fee.

Roth IRA conversions

The tax law does not allow a rollover of 401(k) money directly into a Roth IRA. However, once your retirement savings are in a traditional IRA, you may convert the account to a Roth IRA. You may convert your traditional IRA to a Roth IRA if your modified adjusted gross income (which does not include the traditional IRA balance) does not exceed $100,000 and you file a joint return if you are married.

Roth IRAs are attractive because Roth IRA withdrawals, unlike traditional IRA withdrawals, are not taxed if all requirements are met. However, you must pay income tax on any accumulated earnings and tax-deductible contributions when you do the conversion. This is often called a conversion tax.

Paying the conversion tax may be worthwhile if you will be subject to higher tax rates when you have to withdraw spending money from the account. And there are no required minimum distributions (RMDs) from your Roth IRA during your lifetime.

Under current tax law, the best year to convert a traditional IRA to Roth status may be 2006, unless the schedule of tax rate reductions is changed again. The 2001 federal tax law (the Economic Growth and Tax Relief Reconciliation Act of 2001) reduced the four individual income-tax rates over the 15-percent tax rate. This law is gradually reducing the previous 28-percent, 31-percent, 36-percent, and 38.6-percent tax rates to 25%, 28%, 33%, and 35% by 2006. Thus, the highest individual income tax rate in 2006 is scheduled to be 35%. The schedule for these tax rate reductions is as follows:

	2002–2003	2004–2005	2006 and later years
Former 28% rate becomes:	27%	26%	25%
Former 31% rate becomes:	30%	29%	28%
Former 36% rate becomes:	35%	34%	33%
Former 39.6% rate becomes:	38.6%	37.6%	35%

Unless you expect your modified adjusted gross income to exceed $100,000 in 2006, or unless federal tax rates change again, consider converting your traditional IRA into a Roth IRA in 2006. This may give you time to save other funds to pay the conversion tax.

Hardship withdrawals

Try to avoid having to take a hardship withdrawal. Consider reducing your 401(k) contributions to your employer's match level so that you can save more money for college education, the purchase of a home, and emergencies. That's because hardship withdrawals carry heavy tax costs.

The tax law allows employers to grant hardship withdrawals to 401(k) plan participants, but employers are not required to do so. The tax law recognizes that the following hardships justify early distributions from a 401(k) account:

- Medical expenses previously incurred or about to be incurred by the 401(k) account owner, his or her spouse, or his or her dependent(s).

- Costs related to the purchase of the 401(k) owner's principal residence (not including mortgage payments).

- Payment of expenses of obtaining a post-secondary education for the 401(k) owner, his or her spouse, and his or her dependent(s).

- Payments necessary to prevent eviction from or foreclosure on a mortgage on the participant's principal residence.

Hardship distributions are subject to the 10-percent penalty (unless an exception applies), as well as federal and state income taxes. Therefore, consider taking a 401(k) loan before you take a hardship distribution.

401(k) loans

More than 90 percent of employers let their employees who participate in the company's 401(k) plan borrow money from their 401(k) accounts. These plans generally allow the employees to use their own 401(k) money for the loan and pay the principal and "interest" back to them. But borrowing from your 401(k) account is not as good a deal as it may appear.

Unlike your 401(k) contributions, your 401(k) loan repayments come out of your after-tax income. When you withdraw the repaid amounts after retirement (or convert, indirectly, to a Roth IRA), you will be taxed again.

Leaving your job before you finish the regular loan repayment schedule is bad news. You either have to come up with the cash to repay the loan balance or pay income taxes and the 10-percent penalty on the unpaid balance.

Shielding your 401(k) money from creditors

Do you owe money to an individual, a business, or the government? If so, then you have a creditor. If you have trouble paying off that debt, your creditor might sue you to force you to liquidate your assets to settle the debt.

If it is a commercial debt—such as money you owe to a home-improvement contractor or a professional, such a your doctor—your 401(k) account is protected. A court may not do the following:

- ◆ Freeze your 401(k) account until you pay your debt.
- ◆ Order you or your 401(k) plan to take money out of your account to pay your debt.
- ◆ Set aside any part of the money in your 401(k) account to pay your debt when you withdraw money years from now.

However, if you owe money to the federal government, your spouse, your former spouse, or your children, a court may force you to take money from your 401(k) account to pay that debt. This includes money you owe for alimony, child support, and federal income taxes.

Everyone else, including state and local tax authorities, can't get your 401(k) money. So, in a situation when your 401(k) is protected from creditors, you may ignore anyone who pressures you to take money out of your 401(k) account.

When you are retiring or changing jobs, you may have the chance to take your money out of your 401(k) account or roll it over into a traditional IRA. If you do, the money might not be protected from creditors any more. If you have money troubles, consider leaving your money in your 401(k) account, if your employer will let you.

At some point, you may decide to file for bankruptcy. In bankruptcy, certain assets may be liquidated to pay some off certain debts, whereas certain other assets are protected.

When you declare bankruptcy, your IRA may become vulnerable to creditors' claims. Whether your IRA is protected depends on state law. Consider asking a local bankruptcy attorney as to whether your IRA would be at risk.

Divorce-related distributions

When a married couple gets a divorce, the balance in the husband's and the wife's 401(k) accounts are included in the division of marital property. However, 401(k) accounts are unlike most other marital assets because they are tax-deferred. For the purpose of a marital property division, the fair market value of a 401(k) account is the balance of the account reduced by the marginal tax rate of the 401(k) account owner.

> **Example.** A couple that is getting a divorce once bought a house with a current fair market value of $73,000. The wife has a 401(k) account, to which she starting contributing during the marriage, with a current balance of $100,000. The wife is in the 27-percent federal tax bracket. (Assume no state taxes.) The postponed taxes on the 401(k) account balance is $27,000 (27% x $100,000). Therefore, the value of the wife's 401(k) account for the purpose of the division of marital property is $73,000 ($100,000–$27,000).

In a division of marital property, each item of property can be divided between the spouses. To get a share of one spouse's 401(k) account, the other spouse's attorney will ask the court to issue a Qualified Domestic Relations Order (QDRO). The QDRO (pronounced "kwa-dro") tells the 401(k) plan to divide the account assets between the account owner and the alternate payee (the former spouse). The 401(k) plan may create two subaccounts, one that the original account owner controls and one that the alternate payee controls. In essence, each spouse then owns a separate 401(k) account.

A qualified domestic relations order (QDRO) is a judgment, decree, or court order that relates to the rights of the alternate payee (someone other than the 401(k) owner) to receive benefits from the 401(k) plan and specifies the amount or portion of the 401(k) owner's benefits to be paid to the alternate payee.

Distributions paid under a QDRO to the alternate payee must generally be included in the alternate payee's income. If the participant made any after-tax contributions to the 401(k) account, those contributions are allocated to the alternate payee.

If you receive an eligible rollover distribution under a QDRO as the alternate payee, you may be able to roll it over tax-free into a traditional IRA or another qualified plan. If you take the distribution but do not roll it over, the distribution is taxable to you. However, you do not have to pay the 10-percent penalty.

Once a QDRO is issued, the 401(k) plan has 18 months to rule on its validity. The alternate payee's attorney may ask that the 401(k) account be frozen so that the participant can't take a 401(k) loan or roll it over into an IRA before the order is accepted as qualified.

Once the 401(k) plan accepts the QDRO, the alternate payee may:

◆ Roll the money over into his or her own IRA.
◆ Leave the money with the 401(k) plan in a separate account.
◆ Take the money in a lump-sum distribution.

The first two alternatives—the IRA rollover and staying in the 401(k) plan—are not subject to taxes or penalties. If the alternate payee takes the lump-sum distribution, he or she will be subject to income tax. However, the 10-percent penalty does not apply to a QDRO distribution.

Here is one way to avoid a QDRO. Oftentimes, one spouse or the other is emotionally attached to a certain piece of marital property, such as a house. The chance to take 100-percent ownership of the house can serve as a powerful bargaining chip in a divorce negotiation.

If you want to keep all or most of your 401(k) money, don't be afraid to give up your share of a house or other marital asset. How the 401(k) account is handled in the divorce may make a big difference in your financial future.

Ensuring long-lived financial security

Fifty years ago, few individuals had to worry about long-term financial security, because few could expect to live long after they retired. Now, living 30 or more years in retirement is common. One of the biggest problems facing today's 401(k) investors is that they may outlive their retirement savings.

The solution to this problem may be to turn your retirement savings into annuities. An annuity is a contract with a life insurance company or other financial institution to pay you a regular income for life.

When you retire, you may roll over your 401(k) money into an individual retirement annuity. Alternatively, your 401(k) plan may be able to annuitize your 401(k) savings.

Annuities have a big advantage over other ways to live off of your 401(k) savings: lifetime income. The insurance company that pays the annuity to you is betting that you will die before your life expectancy. You are betting that you will outlive your life expectancy. No matter who is right, you can rest assured that your money will not run out.

The downside of annuities is that they are essentially irrevocable: Once you buy one, you can't change your mind. Annuities are also vulnerable to inflation and the insolvency of the insurance company. Fortunately, there are ways to minimize the risks of inflation and insolvency.

When you buy an annuity, you should buy it from an insurance company that will stay in business for at least as long as the rest of your life. You have the best chance of working with a financially strong company by paying close attention to the credit ratings of insurance companies.

Credit rating services include A.M. Best, Duff & Phelps, Moody's, Standard & Poor's, and Weiss Research. You should be able to find this ratings information in your public library or on the Internet. Look at several insurance companies and several ratings for each company.

Another way to reduce the risk that an insurance company insolvency will erase your financial security is to buy your annuities from more than one company. Then, if one company goes under, you are still receiving annuity payments from the companies that are still in business.

To hedge against the risk of inflation, consider buying a variable annuity instead of a fixed annuity. With a variable annuity, your money is invested in stocks and other equities. The income you receive will depend on the investment results. The disadvantage of a variable annuity is that the interest rate is not guaranteed.

Some individuals see another risk in buying annuities: that you'll die soon after you buy the annuity. Then the insurance company would get to keep money that would have gone to your heirs. If premature death is your concern, consider buying a life annuity with term certain or a joint and survivor annuity.

With a life annuity with term certain, you receive income for the rest of your life. But if you die before you receive a specific number of payments, your beneficiary will receive the balance of the number of income payments that you choose.

With joint and survivor annuity, income payments are received for as long as either of two people is alive. See Appendix C for an example of a joint and survivor life expectancy table. Upon the death of either person, income continues as a percentage of the original amount. Common percentages chosen for the survivor are 50 percent, 66 2/3 percent, and 100 percent.

401(k) Distribution Do's and Don'ts

- DO roll over your 401(k) account balance into a traditional IRA when you leave your employer, unless you might file for bankruptcy and IRAs are not protected from creditors in your state.

- DO take steps to avoid administrative delays when you roll over your 401(k) account balance.

- DO avoid tax withholding by choosing a direct rollover.

- DON'T take a hardship withdrawal if there is any way to avoid it.

- DON'T take a 401(k) loan unless absolutely necessary.

- DON'T be afraid to give up your share of a house or other marital asset during divorce negotiations so you can keep as much of your retirement savings as possible.

- DON'T worry about outliving your retirement savings. Consider buying an annuity.

Chapter 7

Preserving Your 401(k) for Your Heirs

"Death and taxes and childbirth! There's never any convenient time for any of them!"

—Margaret Mitchell, *Gone With the Wind*

ALTHOUGH SOME 401(k) ACCOUNT OWNERS FEAR that they won't have enough money for a comfortable retirement, other 401(k) account owners may not need their money to cover their living expenses. Such individuals often prefer to preserve their 401(k) money for their heirs.

So, what's stopping them? Two things: required minimum distributions (RMDs) and taxes.

Your required minimum distributions

The government won't let your money stay in your 401(k) account forever. Generally speaking, you must begin to take distributions from your 401(k) plan by April 1st of the year that follows the later of (1) the year in which you reach age 70½ or (2) the year in which you retire.

Under the tax law, this is your "required beginning date." However, your 401(k) plan may require you to begin to receive distributions by April 1st of the year that follows the year in which you reach age 70½, even if you have not retired.

Moreover, if you are a 5-percent owner of the company that sponsors your 401(k) plan, you must begin to take your RMDs by April 1 of the year that follows the year in which you reach age 70½, even if you are still working for the company. You are a 5-percent owner if you own (or are considered to own) more than 5 percent of at least one of the following:

- The outstanding stock of the company.
- The total voting power of all stock of the company.
- The capital or profits interest in the company.

How do you know when you are 70½ years old? It's simple: You reach age 70½ exactly six months after your 70th birthday. So, for example, if your 70th birthday is on June 30, 2003, you turn age 70½ on December 30, 2003. If your 70th birthday is on July 1, 2003, you reach age 70½ on January 1, 2004.

After your starting year for RMDs, you must receive the RMD for each year by December 31st of that year. (The starting year is the year in which you reach age 70½ or retire, whichever applies in determining your required beginning date.) If you don't take an RMD in your starting year, you must take two RMDs in the following year (one by April 1st and one by December 31st).

> **Example.** You retired with a 401(k) account in 2001. You reached age 70½ on August 20, 2002. You must receive your RMD for 2002 from your 401(k) account by April 1, 2003. You must receive the RMD for 2003 by December 31, 2003.

If you receive your first two RMDs in the same year, as in the previous example, you will have to pay income taxes on both RMDs in the same year. "Bunching" two RMDs into the same year may put you into a higher tax bracket. To avoid the "bunching" problem, consider taking your first RMD in the year you turn 70½, even though your required beginning date isn't until April 1 of the next year.

The rules for calculating your RMD amount were recently simplified. Now your RMDs are generally based on your account balance at the end of the previous year and your age and the current year. Simply divide your year-end account balance by the distribution period for your age, as provided in an IRS Uniform Table. Figure 7-1 (on page 102) shows the IRS's chart for the distribution period (in years) for a 401(k) account owner's required minimum distributions after age 70 ½.

> **Example.** In 2003, Al reaches age 74 and his wife Betty turns age 71. Al's 401(k) account balance at the end of 2002 was $600,000. According to the Uniform Table, Al's distribution period in 2003 is 23.8 years. Therefore, Al's 2003 RMD is $25,210, which is $600,000 divided by 23.8.

However, if your spouse is your sole beneficiary and is more than 10 years younger than you are, your distribution period is provided in a separate IRS table for joint and survivor life expectancy. (Please see Appendix C.) To use this table, locate one spouse's age on the vertical axis and the other spouse's age on the horizontal axis. The number that is at the intersection of the two ages is the distribution period for the 401(k) account owner.

> **Example.** In 2003, Carl turns 74 years old. His wife Donna, who is the sole beneficiary of Carl's 401(k) account, becomes 60 years old. Carl's 401(k) account balance at the end of 2002 is $600,000. According to the joint life and survivor expectancy table, Carl's distribution period is 26.6. Therefore, Carl's RMD for 2003 is $22,556 ($600,000 / 26.6).

Figure 7-1. Uniform Table for 401(k) Account Owners

Current Age	Years	Current Age	Years
70	27.4	93	9.6
71	26.5	94	9.1
72	25.6	95	8.6
73	24.7	96	8.1
74	23.8	97	7.6
75	22.9	98	7.1
76	22.0	99	6.7
77	21.2	100	6.3
78	20.3	101	5.9
79	19.5	102	5.5
80	18.7	103	5.2
81	17.9	104	4.9
82	17.1	105	4.5
83	16.3	106	4.2
84	15.5	107	3.9
85	14.8	108	3.7
86	14.1	109	3.4
87	13.4	110	3.1
88	12.7	111	2.9
89	12.0	112	2.6
90	11.4	113	2.4
91	10.8	114	2.1
92	10.2	115+	1.0

Source: Treasury Regulations.

Note: This table is used to determine a 401(k) account owner's RMDs when the 401(k) account owner's spouse is not the sole beneficiary or when the spouse is the sole beneficiary but is not more than 10 years younger than the 401(k) account owner.

Other rules may apply if you receive distributions from your retirement plan in the form of an annuity. Your plan administrator should be able to give you information about these rules.

State income taxes

Your RMD distributions are taxable not only on your federal income-tax return, but often also on your state income-tax return. However, the following states have no income tax:

- ◆ Alaska.
- ◆ Florida.
- ◆ Nevada.
- ◆ South Dakota.
- ◆ Texas.
- ◆ Washington.
- ◆ Wyoming.

Most of the 43 states that impose income taxes exempt at least some retirement income. Pennsylvania does not tax retirement income at all, including Social Security benefits, IRA distributions, and pensions. Kentucky, Michigan, New Jersey, New York, and South Carolina have generous—but not complete—retirement income exemptions. Mississippi exempts all public and private pension income. Consult a tax accountant for more information.

Florida imposes an annual intangibles tax on the value of certain assets, including stocks, bonds, and mutual funds. However, Florida's intangibles tax exempts 401(k) accounts and IRAs, as well as money market accounts, certificates of deposit, annuities, cash-value life insurance, and Florida bonds.

If you are thinking about retiring to a state that does not tax 401(k) distributions, don't assume that your previous state can't tax your distributions from your tax-deferred accounts. Simply living in one state at the time of the distribution does not stop another state from taxing income that was earned there.

The issue is whether or not you have taken enough steps to abandon residence in one state and to establish legal residence in your retirement state. Every state has its own rules, which can often be found in the instructions to the state's income-tax forms.

Generally speaking, the states' rules compare the personal and financial connection to the old state with the connections to the new state. States also consider the number of days present in each state and the maintenance of a home in a state.

If you maintain homes in two or more states, you may want to establish legal residence in the state with the most favorable tax laws. Taking the following steps will help (but will not guarantee) you establish residence in the state that you prefer:

- Use and maintain your home in your preferred state more than your home(s) in other state(s).

- If you are working, conduct your business primarily in your preferred state.

- Locate items with sentimental or monetary value, such as family heirlooms, artworks, and personal collections, in your preferred state.

- Be involved in community, religious, civic, and social activities more in your preferred state than in any other state.

- Use the address of your home in your preferred state for your bank account statements, credit card bills, federal income-tax return, and family and business correspondence.

- Obtain your driver's license in your preferred state.

- Register to vote in your preferred state.

- Use lawyers, doctors, accountants, brokers, and other professionals primarily in your preferred state.

- Recite your preferred state as your domicile in your will and other legal documents.

Roth IRA conversion

One way to eliminate RMDs is to roll over your 401(k) money into a traditional IRA and then convert the traditional IRA into a Roth IRA. There are no RMDs from your Roth IRA during your lifetime.

You may convert your traditional IRA to a Roth IRA if your modified adjusted gross income (which does not include the traditional IRA balance) does not exceed $100,000 and you file a joint return if you are married. However, you must pay income tax on any accumulated earnings and tax-deductible contributions when you do the conversion. Paying the conversion tax may be worthwhile if you will be subject to higher tax rates when you have to withdraw spending money from the account.

Another reason why Roth IRAs are attractive is that Roth IRA withdrawals, unlike traditional IRA withdrawals, are not taxed if all requirements are met. (Refer back to Chapter 6 for more information.)

The tax-free nature of Roth IRA contributions applies to your heirs as well. Note that nonspouses who inherit 401(k) accounts or traditional IRAs may not convert them to Roth IRAs.

Naming your beneficiary

To pass on your 401(k) account, you must specifically name (on a special beneficiary form that your 401(k) plan provides) the individuals you want to receive the money. If you try to name the beneficiary of your 401(k) account in your will, it won't work.

Generally speaking, 401(k) plans require that you designate your spouse as your beneficiary, unless he or she signs a waiver. Upon inheriting your 401(k) account, your surviving spouse may roll over your 401(k) account balance into a traditional IRA in your spouse's name. This spousal rollover is tax-free.

Under new tax rules, naming someone other than your spouse as your 401(k) beneficiary—no matter what that beneficiary's age—won't affect your RMDs. However, naming a nonspouse beneficiary who is much younger than you may stretch out the life of your 401(k) account because, if you die after your required beginning date, that individual's RMDs are based on his or her life expectancy. (Please see Figure 7-2 on pages 107 and 108.)

> **Example.** Elaine, age 33 in 2003, inherited a 401(k) account from her father, who died at the age of 75 in 2002. At the end of 2002, the account balance was $1,500,000. According to the IRS's life expectancy table for inherited accounts, Elaine's life expectancy is 50.4 years. Therefore, Elaine's RMD from her father's 401(k) account is $29,762, which is $1,500,000 divided by 50.4.

If you die before your required beginning date, your entire 401(k) account must be distributed under one of the following rules:

- ◆ Rule 1. The distributions must be completed by December 31st of the fifth year following the year of your death.
- ◆ Rule 2. The distributions must be made in annual amounts over the life expectancy of the designated beneficiary.

The terms of your 401(k) plan determine which of these two rules applies. If your 401(k) plan lets you or your beneficiary choose the rule that applies, this choice must be made by the earliest date a distribution would be required under either of the rules. Generally, this date is December 31st of the year following the year of your death.

Figure 7-2. Single Life Table for
Inherited 401(k) Accounts

Age at inheritance	Life expectancy in years	Age at inheritance	Life expectancy in years
0	82.4	28	55.3
1	81.6	29	54.3
2	80.6	30	53.3
3	79.7	31	52.4
4	78.7	32	51.4
5	77.7	33	50.4
6	76.7	34	49.4
7	75.8	35	48.5
8	74.8	36	47.5
9	73.8	37	46.5
10	72.8	38	45.6
11	71.8	39	44.6
12	70.8	40	43.6
13	69.9	41	42.7
14	68.9	42	41.7
15	67.9	43	40.7
16	66.9	44	39.8
17	66	45	38.8
18	65	46	37.9
19	64	47	37
20	63	48	36
21	62.1	49	35.1
22	61.1	50	34.2
23	60.1	51	33.3
24	59.1	52	32.3
25	58.2	53	31.4
26	57.2	54	30.5
27	56.2	55	29.6

(continued on next page)

Figure 7-2. Single Life Table for Inherited 401(k) Accounts (cont'd.)

Age at inheritance	Life expectancy in years	Age at inheritance	Life expectancy in years
56	28.7	85	7.6
57	27.9	86	7.1
58	27	87	6.7
59	26.1	88	6.3
60	25.2	89	5.9
61	24.4	90	5.5
62	23.5	91	5.2
63	22.7	92	4.9
64	21.8	93	4.6
65	21	94	4.3
66	20.2	95	4.1
67	19.4	96	3.8
68	18.6	97	3.6
69	17.8	98	3.4
70	17	99	3.1
71	16.3	100	2.9
72	15.5	101	2.7
73	14.8	102	2.5
74	14.1	103	2.3
75	13.4	104	2.1
76	12.7	105	1.9
77	12.1	106	1.7
78	11.4	107	1.5
79	10.8	108	1.4
80	10.2	109	1.2
81	9.7	110	1.1
82	9.1	111+	1
83	8.6		
84	8.1		

Source: Treasury Regulations.

If you or your beneficiary do not choose either rule and the plan does not specify the one that applies, the distribution must be made under Rule 2 if you have named a beneficiary and under Rule 1 if you have not named a beneficiary.

RMDs under Rule 2 generally must begin by December 31st of the year following the year of your death. However, if your spouse is the beneficiary, the RMDs don't have to start until December 31st of the year you would have reached age 70½, if later.

Some 401(k) plans don't want the administrative hassles of distributing RMDs to beneficiaries, especially nonspouse beneficiaries. The tax law provides 401(k) plans with the flexibility to make distributions that are faster according to the RMD rules. So, some 401(k) plans issue a lump-sum distribution check to the beneficiary shortly after the 401(k) account owner dies.

A nonspouse beneficiary may not roll over such a lump-sum distribution into a traditional IRA. Therefore, the full amount of the 401(k) account balance becomes taxable to the beneficiary in one year. You can find out your 401(k) plan's policy by checking the summary plan description.

> **Example.** George, a single individual with no other income, inherits a $600,000 401(k) account. The 401(k) plan's policy is to distribute the entire 401(k) account to a nonspouse beneficiary shortly after the death of the 401(k) account owner. In the year of the distribution, George suddenly becomes subject to the highest federal income-tax rate. His federal income tax liability in that year is $205,986. This leaves George with only $394,015 after federal income taxes.

Some 401(k) account owners prefer to name a charity, a trust, or their estate as their alternate beneficiary—or even as the primary beneficiary. Such strategies have advantages and disadvantages. Consult an estate-planning professional for more information.

Estate taxes

Generally, RMDs and other distributions from your 401(k) account, whether made to you or your beneficiary, are subject to income tax. What's more, the balance of your 401(k) account is included in your estate for estate tax purposes when you die.

Fortunately, the property that you pass to your spouse and to charity at your death is exempt from estate tax. And the federal government grants some pretty generous exemption amounts for the value of property that you give to others, such as your children. The schedule of federal estate-tax exemption amounts is as follows:

2003	$1 million
2004–2005	$1.5 million
2006–2008	$2 million
2009	$3.5 million
2010	Estate tax repealed
2011	$1 million

Because of a quirk in the federal tax law, the estate-tax exemption amount jumps to $3.5 million in 2009, the federal estate tax is repealed for 2010 only, and the tax is reinstated in 2011 with an exemption amount of $1 million. And this quirky schedule is subject to change.

Less likely to change in the next few years are the types of property that would be includable in your estate for estate-tax purposes. In addition to your 401(k) account, these assets would include, among others:

- ◆ Real estate.
- ◆ Cash and marketable securities.
- ◆ Traditional and Roth IRAs.
- ◆ Personal property, such as vehicles, furniture, and jewelry.

◆ A life insurance death benefit that is payable when you
  die, if you are the owner of the life insurance policy.

The value of each piece of your property would be added together
to determine the total value of your estate. Then the marital deduction, the charitable deduction, and the exclusion amount would generally be subtracted. If there is any amount left over, that amount is
subject to federal estate tax.

> **Example.** Kyle, a widower, has a $500,000 life insurance
> policy, a house worth $200,000, and a 401(k) account with a
> balance of $300,000. Kyle's estate is worth $1 million for
> estate tax purposes. If Kyle dies in 2003 and leaves his en-
> tire estate to his daughter, his $1 million federal exclusion
> amount reduces his taxable estate to zero.

As you figure out whether your estate would be taxed by the federal government, keep your state's estate taxes in mind, too. These
days, many jurisdictions have an estate-tax exemption amount that is
lower than the federal estate-tax exemption amount. They are:

◆ District of Columbia.

◆ Kansas.

◆ Massachusetts.

◆ Minnesota.

◆ Nebraska.

◆ New Jersey.

◆ New York.

◆ Oklahoma.

◆ Oregon.

◆ Pennsylvania.

◆ Rhode Island.

- ◆ Washington (state).
- ◆ Wisconsin.

Estate-planning Tips for Your 401(k) Account

- ◆ To maximize the value of your 401(k) account that you leave to your heirs, consider taking only the required minimum distributions (RMDs) from your account.

- ◆ Choose your 401(k) beneficiary carefully. That decision may affect your beneficiary's RMDs and your estate taxes.

- ◆ Consider moving to a state that will not tax your 401(k) distributions and other retirement income. If you do, take steps to abandon legal residence in your old state.

- ◆ Consider rolling over your 401(k) account into a traditional IRA and then converting the traditional IRA into a Roth IRA.

Chapter 8

Seeking Professional Financial Advice

"Never trust the advice of a man in difficulties."

—Aesop

MANAGING YOUR 401(K) ACCOUNT CAN BE a lot of work. Certainly it is something you can do on your own, but maybe you would like to talk to a professional now and then.

Financial advisors are in the business of giving advice about personal finance to clients. There are many types of advisors who can help you develop a personal financial plan and manage your hard-earned 401(k) money.

One kind of financial advisor might give you advice only about investing in stocks, bonds, or mutual funds. Such an advisor may call himself or herself a financial planner, but essentially he or she is selling investments.

Another kind of financial advisor assesses every aspect of your financial life—including saving, investments, insurance, taxes, retirement, and estate planning. He or she may also help you develop a detailed strategy or financial plan for meeting all your financial goals.

Before you start working with any kind of financial advisor, you should know exactly what you are getting. You show know what services the advisor can deliver, any limitations on what he or she can recommend, what services you're paying for, and how much those services will cost you.

If you want someone to help you just with your 401(k) account, you may have trouble finding someone. Commission-based advisors can't make money from assets that are held in a 401(k) account. (They would be happy to help you with an IRA rollover, though.) If you have to—or want to—keep your money in you 401(k) account, you may have to look for a fee-based financial advisor.

Be sure to meet potential advisors face to face to make sure you get along. In addition, check out the professional you choose with the appropriate securities regulator or professional association.

Regulations and credentials

Certain financial advisors must register with either the Securities and Exchange Commission (SEC) or the securities agency for the state in which they do business. For the most part, advisors who manage $25 million or more in client assets must register with the SEC. If they manage less than $25 million, they must register with the state securities agency in the state where they have their principal place of business.

Most investment advisors must fill out a form called "Form ADV." They must file their ADVs with either the SEC or the state securities agency in the state where they have their principal place of business, depending on the amount of assets they manage.

The ADV consists of two parts. Part I contains information about the advisor's education, business, and whether he or she previously had problems with regulators or clients. Part II outlines the advisor's services, fees, and strategies. Before you hire someone to be your advisor, ask for and carefully read both parts of the ADV.

You can get copies of Form ADVs from the advisor, your state securities regulator, or the SEC, depending on the advisor. You can find out how to get in touch with your state securities regulator through the North American Securities Administrators Association by calling 1-202-737-0900. Ask your state securities regulator whether it has had any complaints about the advisor.

If the SEC registers the investment advisor, you can get the Form ADV by contacting the SEC (Office of Public Reference, 450 5th Street, NW, Room 1300, Washington, D.C. 20549-0102; phone: 1-202-942-8090; fax: 1-202-628-9001; e-mail: *publicinfo@sec.gov*).

Although some investment advisors and financial planners have credentials such as CFP™ (certified financial planner™) or CFA (chartered financial analyst), financial advisors are not required to by federal or state laws. Although the SEC does not require a proficiency exam, many states do require their advisors and representatives to pass a proficiency exam or meet other requirements.

If the professional you're considering claims to be a CFP™, consider contacting the Certified Financial Planner Board of Standards to see if the professional is indeed a CFP and whether the professional's credential has been suspended or revoked by the Board. You can also call the Board at 1-888-237-6275 to obtain other disciplinary information about the professional.

DILBERT reprinted by permission of United Feature Syndicate, Inc.

Investment advisors and financial planners may come from many different educational and professional backgrounds. Before you hire a financial advisor, be sure to ask about his or her background. If the advisor has a credential that you haven't heard of, ask him or her what it means and what it takes to earn it.

Also find out what organization issued the credential. Then contact the organization to verify whether the professional you're considering did, in fact, earn the credential and whether the professional remains in good standing with the organization.

How do financial advisors get paid?

Before you start working with any financial advisor—whether he or she be a stockbroker, a financial planner, or other advisor—you should find out and make sure you understand how that individual gets paid. A financial advisor may be paid in any one or more of the following ways:

- A fixed fee.
- A percentage of the value of the assets he or she manages for you.
- An hourly fee for the time he or she spends working for you.
- A commission on the securities he or she sells.

Each compensation method has potential benefits and possible drawbacks, depending on your individual needs. Ask the financial advisors you interview to explain the differences to you before you do business with them, and get several opinions before making your decision.

Investment advice from your 401(k) plan

Until recently, federal law discouraged employers from offering 401(k) participants any specific investment advice. That's because employers would have been legally responsible if their advice resulted in investment losses. Employers could provide general investment education, as long as they avoided mentioning specific investment alternatives.

In December 2001, the U.S. Department of Labor said that 401(k) plans may give specific investment advice to participants. This advice can be tailored to 401(k) investors' individual profiles.

The Department of Labor requires that the financial advisor be independent of the service provider that sells the 401(k) plan's investment alternatives. The financial advisor's fees may not be linked to his or her specific investment advice in any way. And the 401(k) investors must still make the final investment decisions.

Congress is working on legislation that would encourage more employers to give 401(k) advice. But if the legislation allows 401(k) service providers that sell investments to provide the advice, instead of independent financial advisors, watch out. Who do you think the advisors will look out for: your interests or theirs?

Also, don't assume that financial advice sponsored by your 401(k) plan will be free. You should expect your employer to pass the cost of providing the advice on to you through higher 401(k) management fees. Face-to-face financial advice is expensive. Telephone conferences may be less expensive.

Some observers say that 401(k) investment advice may not be the answer to anemic retirement savings. They claim that the financial services industry is biased toward mutual funds with large management fees. And all of the investment strategy in the world won't make up for overspending and saving too little.

Whether you use an advisor provided by your 401(k) plan or you find someone on your own, the advice you get should be trustworthy.

This means that you feel comfortable that your advisor is looking out for your best interests above anything else.

Questions to Ask When Choosing a Financial Advisor

- What experience do you have, especially with individuals similar to me?

- Where did you go to school?

- What is your recent employment history?

- What licenses do you hold? Are you registered with the SEC or a state?

- What products and services do you offer?

- Can you recommend only a limited number of products or services to me? If so, why?

- How are you paid for your services? What is your usual hourly rate, flat fee, or commission?

- Has any government regulator ever disciplined you for unethical or improper conduct?

- Has a client who was not happy with the work you did ever sued you?

- For registered investment advisors only: Will you give me a copy of both parts of your Form ADV?

Enron: From "Bargain" to Bankruptcy in 67 Days

O N SEPTEMBER 26, 2001, ENRON CORPORATION's chairman, Kenneth Lay, encouraged Enron employees to buy stock in the company, calling it a "bargain." Sixty-seven days later, on December 2, Enron filed for bankruptcy—one of the largest U.S. bankruptcies ever—and left Enron employees and other investors with stock that was suddenly almost worthless. What happened?

Enron thrived in the deregulated energy trading market of the 1990s. In 2000, it rose to the number-seven spot in revenues on the Fortune 500. Its financial statements showed big profits and a healthy net worth. In reality, it had neither.

Enron was involved in thousands of hidden partnerships, with names that were borrowed from popular movies, such as JEDI, Braveheart, Raptor, and Chewco (after the character Chewbacca the Wookie in Star Wars). Advised by law firms and accounting firms, Enron's executives believed that organizing the partnerships in certain ways would allow the partnerships to be treated as separate businesses with no reporting responsibility except to the IRS.

In this way, certain debts that Enron executives didn't want investors to know about could be shifted to the partnerships and effectively disappear. Less debt on Enron's financial statements would make the company appear strong. And that would support the market price of Enron stock.

Enron's main tactic was to use *special purpose entities*. These entities—usually partnerships—were created and owned almost entirely by Enron. As long as an outside investor contributed at least 3 percent of the start-up cash, they could be treated as independent of Enron for accounting purposes.

Enron's first partnerships were very successful. Beginning in 1993, an oil partnership with the California Public Employees' Retirement System (CalPERS) was making money. This partnership was called JEDI (short for Joint Energy Development Investments). When CalPERS wanted to get out of the deal, Enron created Chewco, another 97-percent owned partnership, to take over CalPERS's share of JEDI.

In the late 1990s, Enron began to lose money. Because Enron executives could profit from their Enron stock options only as long as Enron stock did well, they needed to keep its stock price from collapsing. Enron needed to look as if it had fewer financial problems than it really did.

Enron sold its assets to the partnerships for cash paid for by the partnerships from money borrowed from banks and investors. Enron then claimed the proceeds of the asset sales as pure profit, by neglecting to deduct the value of the asset it no longer had.

Managers in Enron's finance department were often provided a list of Enron assets and told to sell some of them to the partnerships. These assets included everything from power plants to stock in start-up companies.

In the typical deal, a bank or other investor lent money to the newly created partnership to finance the purchase of Enron's assets. The partnership, in turn, gave the money to Enron in exchange for the assets. The sale of Enron assets counted as income to Enron. The debt, on the partnership books, did not show up anywhere except within the private halls of Enron and its accountant's offices.

The practice of selling assets to outside partnerships ensured that Enron would maintain its good credit rating, save money, and support the price of Enron stock. But employees joked that there would eventually be no more assets left to sell.

The basic idea was simple. Suppose the asset to be sold was 100 shares of GE stock. Each share would be divided into two parts: one was the "control interest" and the other was the "economic interest." Enron would sell only the economic interest to a partnership. An economic interest is the right to receive the income from assets. Maintaining the control interest allowed Enron to continue to show the asset on its balance sheet.

However, the asset was rarely as easy to value as 100 shares of another public company's stock. Because there wasn't a real outside buyer, Enron managers decided the price of the economic interest themselves and had that price approved by its outside accounting firm.

Next, a bank, insurance company, or other major lender lent the partnership up to 97 percent of the money needed to purchase the asset. Sometimes Enron stock would be used to guarantee the loan, a form of collateral. However, the risk that Enron stock could be diluted, if such new shares had to be issued, was never disclosed to Enron shareholders.

Over time, the partnership made the principal and interest payments to the lender. If it couldn't repay the loan, Enron was obligated to do so, but that obligation didn't appear on Enron's financial statements. The important thing for Enron was that it got to report the proceeds of the sale of the asset as earnings.

Why didn't Enron just borrow the money itself without going through a partnership? Because if the loan were an obligation of an "independent" partnership, it wouldn't count as a debt on Enron's balance sheet.

Why didn't Enron just sell the assets outright? Enron needed to maintain control of the assets to show a strong balance sheet. If the asset was a power plant, Enron needed it to operate its businesses. If it was private shares of another company, Enron might be forbidden to sell them.

Enron also formed two other partnerships, LJM1 and LJM2, in 1999 using its own cash and stock. Pension funds, banks, and other investors also invested millions of dollars in the two partnerships.

Enron's chief financial officer, Andrew Fastow, was the managing partner for both entities. The fact that Fastow acted as both buyer and seller in these transactions was a serious conflict of interest.

LJM1 and LJM2 were intended to become sources of money to buy assets from Enron. Between June 1999 and September 2001, Enron and its affiliates completed 24 transactions with LJM1 and LJM2, including buying and selling productive assets, purchasing debt or equity interests, and selling the rights to buy or sell shares of stock at prearranged prices.

As Enron began to crumble in the fall of 2001, the company repeatedly pointed to its strong earnings history, as evidenced by the $1.5 billion profit it had reported over the previous 15 months. But an internal investigation released in February 2002 said that as much as $1 billion of that profit was an illusion, created by the partnerships that used the faulty—possibly illegal—accounting procedures.

A month after its troubles began, the company took $586 million in after-tax profits off its books. The February 2002 report showed that Enron should have taken off another $1 billion in pre-tax profits, cutting its reported profits by an additional 72 percent over that time.

A key point: To qualify as "independent" from Enron for accounting purposes, a partnership merely had to have an outside partner who invested at least 3 percent of the total start-up cash. But in some cases, Enron allegedly lent that money to the outside partners. In that case, Enron was cheating on the 3-percent rule. So the partnerships should never have been treated as separate businesses for accounting purposes.

That's what happened with Chewco, JEDI, and LJM1. After the third quarter of 2001, Enron announced that Chewco and JEDI's financial losses should have been included in Enron's books, beginning in November 1997. And a subsidiary of the LJM1 partnership should have consolidated its losses into the company's financial statements in 1999.

When Enron was forced to restate its earnings in the third quarter of 2001 to include some of the debt in those partnerships, its whole house of cards started to fall. As debt from other sources also surfaced, credit-reporting agencies downgraded Enron's bond rating. For a trading company such as Enron, that was fatal, because the ability to borrow at favorable interest rates is critical to its profitability in the low-margin energy brokerage business.

Many large companies use special purpose entities. They are legal, provided the other accounting rules that allow for adequate disclosure are followed. But Enron's intercompany transactions were out of the ordinary, even for a company of Enron's size. The earnings restatements in late 2001 alerted Wall Street to Enron's accounting shenanigans.

Eventually, Wall Street and the SEC started asking questions. The company's bond rating fell to junk bond status and the price of Enron stock tumbled. A potential merger with another company fell apart on November 28, 2001. Enron was forced to file for bankruptcy on December 2, 2001. It immediately laid off 4,000 of its 20,000 employees.

By the end of 2002, former CFO Andrew Fastow had been indicted on 78 counts of fraud, money laundering, and conspiracy. Fastow's key aide, Michael Kopper, had pleaded guilty to criminal charges related to his work at Enron.

Tax Advantages of Employer Stock

S ELLING EMPLOYER STOCK AFTER YOU LEAVE your employer is the only exception to the rule that all pre-tax withdrawals from 401(k) plans are taxed at your regular income tax rate.

If employer stock increases in value during the time it's in your 401(k) account, you may be able to postpone paying tax on the gain by withdrawing the stock itself from your account rather than rolling it over to an IRA. If you take out the stock, you will owe income tax only on its value at the time it was added to your account—not the increase in value over the years. You owe no additional taxes (except for taxes on any dividends that you receive) as long as you hold the stock.

> **Example.** Your lump-sum distribution from your 401(k) account includes 1,000 shares of employer stock. When the shares went into your account, they had a total value of $20,000. When the shares were distributed to you, they were

worth $90,000. In the year of distribution, only $20,000 is taxable. The $70,000 appreciation is tax-deferred.

When you sell the shares, the difference between your cost basis and the selling price will be your capital gain or loss.

> **Example.** Six months after you receive the 1,000 shares in the previous example, you sell them for $100,000. Your capital gain is $80,000 ($100,000 selling price minus $20,000 cost basis).

The portion of the gain that is due to the appreciation up to the distribution date is treated as long-term capital gains, no matter how long the shares were held in the plan. Therefore, the previous appreciation would be taxed at the maximum capital gains tax rate of 20 percent (10 percent if you are in the 15-percent tax bracket) instead of the income-tax rate that applies to the rest of your income. The gain that is due to after-distribution appreciation is long-term capital gain only if you held the shares more than one year after you took them out of the 401(k) account.

> **Example.** Continuing the previous example, $70,000 of your gain (the appreciation on the date that you took the shares) is treated as long-term gain and taxed at no more than 20 percent. The remaining $20,000 of gain is treated as short-term gain because you held the stock outside of the 401(k) plan for only six months.

If your lump-sum distribution includes something other than employer stock, you can still postpone paying any taxes on the non-employer stock part by rolling it over into an IRA. Such a rollover doesn't prevent you from postponing taxes on the employer-stock appreciation.

The tax advantages of owning employer stock in your 401(k) account make the decision of whether to keep it more difficult, but those tax advantages are meaningless to individuals who hold worthless stock in their companies. The risk of price volatility and lower returns of a heavy investment in employer stock may outweigh the long-term tax advantages.

Joint and Survivor Life Expectancy Table

THIS CHART MUST BE USED TO calculate the required minimum distribution of a 401(k) owner whose spouse is more than 10 years younger. This chart may also be useful to estimate the joint and survivor life expectancy of a 401(k) owner and a nonspouse beneficiary.

Ages	0	1	2	3	4	5	6	7	8	9
0	90.0	89.5	89.0	88.6	88.2	87.8	87.4	87.1	86.8	86.5
1	89.5	89.0	88.5	88.1	87.6	87.2	86.8	86.5	86.1	85.8
2	89.0	88.5	88.0	87.5	87.1	86.6	86.2	85.8	85.5	85.1
3	88.6	88.1	87.5	87.0	86.5	86.1	85.6	85.2	84.8	84.5
4	88.2	87.6	87.1	86.5	86.0	85.5	85.1	84.6	84.2	83.8
5	87.8	87.2	86.6	86.1	85.5	85.0	84.5	84.1	83.6	83.2
6	87.4	86.8	86.2	85.6	85.1	84.5	84.0	83.5	83.1	82.6
7	87.1	86.5	85.8	85.2	84.6	84.1	83.5	83.0	82.5	82.1
8	86.8	86.1	85.5	84.8	84.2	83.6	83.1	82.5	82.0	81.6
9	86.5	85.8	85.1	84.5	83.8	83.2	82.6	82.1	81.6	81.0
10	86.2	85.5	84.8	84.1	83.5	82.8	82.2	81.6	81.1	80.6

Ages	0	1	2	3	4	5	6	7	8	9
11	85.9	85.2	84.5	83.8	83.1	82.5	81.8	81.2	80.7	80.1
12	85.7	84.9	84.2	83.5	82.8	82.1	81.5	80.8	80.2	79.7
13	85.4	84.7	84.0	83.2	82.5	81.8	81.1	80.5	79.9	79.2
14	85.2	84.5	83.7	83.0	82.2	81.5	80.8	80.1	79.5	78.9
15	85.0	84.3	83.5	82.7	82.0	81.2	80.5	79.8	79.1	78.5
16	84.9	84.1	83.3	82.5	81.7	81.0	80.2	79.5	78.8	78.1
17	84.7	83.9	83.1	82.3	81.5	80.7	80.0	79.2	78.5	77.8
18	84.5	83.7	82.9	82.1	81.3	80.5	79.7	79.0	78.2	77.5
19	84.4	83.6	82.7	81.9	81.1	80.3	79.5	78.7	78.0	77.3
20	84.3	83.4	82.6	81.8	80.9	80.1	79.3	78.5	77.7	77.0
21	84.1	83.3	82.4	81.6	80.8	79.9	79.1	78.3	77.5	76.8
22	84.0	83.2	82.3	81.5	80.6	79.8	78.9	78.1	77.3	76.5
23	83.9	83.1	82.2	81.3	80.5	79.6	78.8	77.9	77.1	76.3
24	83.8	83.0	82.1	81.2	80.3	79.5	78.6	77.8	76.9	76.1
25	83.7	82.9	82.0	81.1	80.2	79.3	78.5	77.6	76.8	75.9
26	83.6	82.8	81.9	81.0	80.1	79.2	78.3	77.5	76.6	75.8
27	83.6	82.7	81.8	80.9	80.0	79.1	78.2	77.4	76.5	75.6
28	83.5	82.6	81.7	80.8	79.9	79.0	78.1	77.2	76.4	75.5
29	83.4	82.6	81.6	80.7	79.8	78.9	78.0	77.1	76.2	75.4
30	83.4	82.5	81.6	80.7	79.7	78.8	77.9	77.0	76.1	75.2
31	83.3	82.4	81.5	80.6	79.7	78.8	77.8	76.9	76.0	75.1

Ages	0	1	2	3	4	5	6	7	8	9
32	83.3	82.4	81.5	80.5	79.6	78.7	77.8	76.8	75.9	75.0
33	83.2	82.3	81.4	80.5	79.5	78.6	77.7	76.8	75.9	74.9
34	83.2	82.3	81.3	80.4	79.5	78.5	77.6	76.7	75.8	74.9
35	83.1	82.2	81.3	80.4	79.4	78.5	77.6	76.6	75.7	74.8
36	83.1	82.2	81.3	80.3	79.4	78.4	77.5	76.6	75.6	74.7
37	83.0	82.2	81.2	80.3	79.3	78.4	77.4	76.5	75.6	74.6
38	83.0	82.1	81.2	80.2	79.3	78.3	77.4	76.4	75.5	74.6
39	83.0	82.1	81.1	80.2	79.2	78.3	77.3	76.4	75.5	74.5
40	82.9	82.1	81.1	80.2	79.2	78.3	77.3	76.4	75.4	74.5
41	82.9	82.0	81.1	80.1	79.2	78.2	77.3	76.3	75.4	74.4
42	82.9	82.0	81.1	80.1	79.1	78.2	77.2	76.3	75.3	74.4
43	82.9	82.0	81.0	80.1	79.1	78.2	77.2	76.2	75.3	74.3
44	82.8	81.9	81.0	80.0	79.1	78.1	77.2	76.2	75.2	74.3
45	82.8	81.9	81.0	80.0	79.1	78.1	77.1	76.2	75.2	74.3
46	82.8	81.9	81.0	80.0	79.0	78.1	77.1	76.1	75.2	74.2
47	82.8	81.9	80.9	80.0	79.0	78.0	77.1	76.1	75.2	74.2
48	82.8	81.9	80.9	80.0	79.0	78.0	77.1	76.1	75.1	74.2
49	82.7	81.8	80.9	79.9	79.0	78.0	77.0	76.1	75.1	74.1
50	82.7	81.8	80.9	79.9	79.0	78.0	77.0	76.0	75.1	74.1
51	82.7	81.8	80.9	79.9	78.9	78.0	77.0	76.0	75.1	74.1
52	82.7	81.8	80.9	79.9	78.9	78.0	77.0	76.0	75.0	74.1

Ages	0	1	2	3	4	5	6	7	8	9
53	82.7	81.8	80.8	79.9	78.9	77.9	77.0	76.0	75.0	74.0
54	82.7	81.8	80.8	79.9	78.9	77.9	76.9	76.0	75.0	74.0
55	82.6	81.8	80.8	79.8	78.9	77.9	76.9	76.0	75.0	74.0
56	82.6	81.7	80.8	79.8	78.9	77.9	76.9	75.9	75.0	74.0
57	82.6	81.7	80.8	79.8	78.9	77.9	76.9	75.9	75.0	74.0
58	82.6	81.7	80.8	79.8	78.8	77.9	76.9	75.9	74.9	74.0
59	82.6	81.7	80.8	79.8	78.8	77.9	76.9	75.9	74.9	74.0
60	82.6	81.7	80.8	79.8	78.8	77.8	76.9	75.9	74.9	73.9
61	82.6	81.7	80.8	79.8	78.8	77.8	76.9	75.9	74.9	73.9
62	82.6	81.7	80.7	79.8	78.8	77.8	76.9	75.9	74.9	73.9
63	82.6	81.7	80.7	79.8	78.8	77.8	76.8	75.9	74.9	73.9
64	82.5	81.7	80.7	79.8	78.8	77.8	76.8	75.9	74.9	73.9
65	82.5	81.7	80.7	79.8	78.8	77.8	76.8	75.8	74.9	73.9
66	82.5	81.7	80.7	79.7	78.8	77.8	76.8	75.8	74.9	73.9
67	82.5	81.7	80.7	79.7	78.8	77.8	76.8	75.8	74.9	73.9
68	82.5	81.6	80.7	79.7	78.8	77.8	76.8	75.8	74.8	73.9
69	82.5	81.6	80.7	79.7	78.8	77.8	76.8	75.8	74.8	73.9
70	82.5	81.6	80.7	79.7	78.8	77.8	76.8	75.8	74.8	73.9
71	82.5	81.6	80.7	79.7	78.7	77.8	76.8	75.8	74.8	73.8
72	82.5	81.6	80.7	79.7	78.7	77.8	76.8	75.8	74.8	73.8
73	82.5	81.6	80.7	79.7	78.7	77.8	76.8	75.8	74.8	73.8

Ages	0	1	2	3	4	5	6	7	8	9
74	82.5	81.6	80.7	79.7	78.7	77.8	76.8	75.8	74.8	73.8
75	82.5	81.6	80.7	79.7	78.7	77.8	76.8	75.8	74.8	73.8
76	82.5	81.6	80.7	79.7	78.7	77.8	76.8	75.8	74.8	73.8
77	82.5	81.6	80.7	79.7	78.7	77.7	76.8	75.8	74.8	73.8
78	82.5	81.6	80.7	79.7	78.7	77.7	76.8	75.8	74.8	73.8
79	82.5	81.6	80.7	79.7	78.7	77.7	76.8	75.8	74.8	73.8
80	82.5	81.6	80.7	79.7	78.7	77.7	76.8	75.8	74.8	73.8
81	82.4	81.6	80.7	79.7	78.7	77.7	76.8	75.8	74.8	73.8
82	82.4	81.6	80.7	79.7	78.7	77.7	76.8	75.8	74.8	73.8
83	82.4	81.6	80.7	79.7	78.7	77.7	76.8	75.8	74.8	73.8
84	82.4	81.6	80.7	79.7	78.7	77.7	76.8	75.8	74.8	73.8
85	82.4	81.6	80.6	79.7	78.7	77.7	76.8	75.8	74.8	73.8
86	82.4	81.6	80.6	79.7	78.7	77.7	76.7	75.8	74.8	73.8
87	82.4	81.6	80.6	79.7	78.7	77.7	76.7	75.8	74.8	73.8
88	82.4	81.6	80.6	79.7	78.7	77.7	76.7	75.8	74.8	73.8
89	82.4	81.6	80.6	79.7	78.7	77.7	76.7	75.8	74.8	73.8
90	82.4	81.6	80.6	79.7	78.7	77.7	76.7	75.8	74.8	73.8
91	82.4	81.6	80.6	79.7	78.7	77.7	76.7	75.8	74.8	73.8
92	82.4	81.6	80.6	79.7	78.7	77.7	76.7	75.8	74.8	73.8
93	82.4	81.6	80.6	79.7	78.7	77.7	76.7	75.8	74.8	73.8
94	82.4	81.6	80.6	79.7	78.7	77.7	76.7	75.8	74.8	73.8

Ages	0	1	2	3	4	5	6	7	8	9
95	82.4	81.6	80.6	79.7	78.7	77.7	76.7	75.8	74.8	73.8
96	82.4	81.6	80.6	79.7	78.7	77.7	76.7	75.8	74.8	73.8
97	82.4	81.6	80.6	79.7	78.7	77.7	76.7	75.8	74.8	73.8
98	82.4	81.6	80.6	79.7	78.7	77.7	76.7	75.8	74.8	73.8
99	82.4	81.6	80.6	79.7	78.7	77.7	76.7	75.8	74.8	73.8
100	82.4	81.6	80.6	79.7	78.7	77.7	76.7	75.8	74.8	73.8
101	82.4	81.6	80.6	79.7	78.7	77.7	76.7	75.8	74.8	73.8
102	82.4	81.6	80.6	79.7	78.7	77.7	76.7	75.8	74.8	73.8
103	82.4	81.6	80.6	79.7	78.7	77.7	76.7	75.8	74.8	73.8
104	82.4	81.6	80.6	79.7	78.7	77.7	76.7	75.8	74.8	73.8
105	82.4	81.6	80.6	79.7	78.7	77.7	76.7	75.8	74.8	73.8
106	82.4	81.6	80.6	79.7	78.7	77.7	76.7	75.8	74.8	73.8
107	82.4	81.6	80.6	79.7	78.7	77.7	76.7	75.8	74.8	73.8
108	82.4	81.6	80.6	79.7	78.7	77.7	76.7	75.8	74.8	73.8
109	82.4	81.6	80.6	79.7	78.7	77.7	76.7	75.8	74.8	73.8
110	82.4	81.6	80.6	79.7	78.7	77.7	76.7	75.8	74.8	73.8
111	82.4	81.6	80.6	79.7	78.7	77.7	76.7	75.8	74.8	73.8
112	82.4	81.6	80.6	79.7	78.7	77.7	76.7	75.8	74.8	73.8
113	82.4	81.6	80.6	79.7	78.7	77.7	76.7	75.8	74.8	73.8
114	82.4	81.6	80.6	79.7	78.7	77.7	76.7	75.8	74.8	73.8
115+	82.4	81.6	80.6	79.7	78.7	77.7	76.7	75.8	74.8	73.8

Ages	10	11	12	13	14	15	16	17	18	19
10	80.0	79.6	79.1	78.7	78.2	77.9	77.5	77.2	76.8	76.5
11	79.6	79.0	78.6	78.1	77.7	77.3	76.9	76.5	76.2	75.8
12	79.1	78.6	78.1	77.6	77.1	76.7	76.3	75.9	75.5	75.2
13	78.7	78.1	77.6	77.1	76.6	76.1	75.7	75.3	74.9	74.5
14	78.2	77.7	77.1	76.6	76.1	75.6	75.1	74.7	74.3	73.9
15	77.9	77.3	76.7	76.1	75.6	75.1	74.6	74.1	73.7	73.3
16	77.5	76.9	76.3	75.7	75.1	74.6	74.1	73.6	73.1	72.7
17	77.2	76.5	75.9	75.3	74.7	74.1	73.6	73.1	72.6	72.1
18	76.8	76.2	75.5	74.9	74.3	73.7	73.1	72.6	72.1	71.6
19	76.5	75.8	75.2	74.5	73.9	73.3	72.7	72.1	71.6	71.1
20	76.3	75.5	74.8	74.2	73.5	72.9	72.3	71.7	71.1	70.6
21	76.0	75.3	74.5	73.8	73.2	72.5	71.9	71.3	70.7	70.1
22	75.8	75.0	74.3	73.5	72.9	72.2	71.5	70.9	70.3	69.7
23	75.5	74.8	74.0	73.3	72.6	71.9	71.2	70.5	69.9	69.3
24	75.3	74.5	73.8	73.0	72.3	71.6	70.9	70.2	69.5	68.9
25	75.1	74.3	73.5	72.8	72.0	71.3	70.6	69.9	69.2	68.5
26	75.0	74.1	73.3	72.5	71.8	71.0	70.3	69.6	68.9	68.2
27	74.8	74.0	73.1	72.3	71.6	70.8	70.0	69.3	68.6	67.9
28	74.6	73.8	73.0	72.2	71.3	70.6	69.8	69.0	68.3	67.6
29	74.5	73.6	72.8	72.0	71.2	70.4	69.6	68.8	68.0	67.3
30	74.4	73.5	72.7	71.8	71.0	70.2	69.4	68.6	67.8	67.1

Ages	10	11	12	13	14	15	16	17	18	19
31	74.3	73.4	72.5	71.7	70.8	70.0	69.2	68.4	67.6	66.8
32	74.1	73.3	72.4	71.5	70.7	69.8	69.0	68.2	67.4	66.6
33	74.0	73.2	72.3	71.4	70.5	69.7	68.8	68.0	67.2	66.4
34	73.9	73.0	72.2	71.3	70.4	69.5	68.7	67.8	67.0	66.2
35	73.9	73.0	72.1	71.2	70.3	69.4	68.5	67.7	66.8	66.0
36	73.8	72.9	72.0	71.1	70.2	69.3	68.4	67.6	66.7	65.9
37	73.7	72.8	71.9	71.0	70.1	69.2	68.3	67.4	66.6	65.7
38	73.6	72.7	71.8	70.9	70.0	69.1	68.2	67.3	66.4	65.6
39	73.6	72.7	71.7	70.8	69.9	69.0	68.1	67.2	66.3	65.4
40	73.5	72.6	71.7	70.7	69.8	68.9	68.0	67.1	66.2	65.3
41	73.5	72.5	71.6	70.7	69.7	68.8	67.9	67.0	66.1	65.2
42	73.4	72.5	71.5	70.6	69.7	68.8	67.8	66.9	66.0	65.1
43	73.4	72.4	71.5	70.6	69.6	68.7	67.8	66.8	65.9	65.0
44	73.3	72.4	71.4	70.5	69.6	68.6	67.7	66.8	65.9	64.9
45	73.3	72.3	71.4	70.5	69.5	68.6	67.6	66.7	65.8	64.9
46	73.3	72.3	71.4	70.4	69.5	68.5	67.6	66.6	65.7	64.8
47	73.2	72.3	71.3	70.4	69.4	68.5	67.5	66.6	65.7	64.7
48	73.2	72.2	71.3	70.3	69.4	68.4	67.5	66.5	65.6	64.7
49	73.2	72.2	71.2	70.3	69.3	68.4	67.4	66.5	65.6	64.6
50	73.1	72.2	71.2	70.3	69.3	68.4	67.4	66.5	65.5	64.6
51	73.1	72.2	71.2	70.2	69.3	68.3	67.4	66.4	65.5	64.5

Ages	10	11	12	13	14	15	16	17	18	19
52	73.1	72.1	71.2	70.2	69.2	68.3	67.3	66.4	65.4	64.5
53	73.1	72.1	71.1	70.2	69.2	68.3	67.3	66.3	65.4	64.4
54	73.1	72.1	71.1	70.2	69.2	68.2	67.3	66.3	65.4	64.4
55	73.0	72.1	71.1	70.1	69.2	68.2	67.2	66.3	65.3	64.4
56	73.0	72.1	71.1	70.1	69.1	68.2	67.2	66.3	65.3	64.3
57	73.0	72.0	71.1	70.1	69.1	68.2	67.2	66.2	65.3	64.3
58	73.0	72.0	71.0	70.1	69.1	68.1	67.2	66.2	65.2	64.3
59	73.0	72.0	71.0	70.1	69.1	68.1	67.2	66.2	65.2	64.3
60	73.0	72.0	71.0	70.0	69.1	68.1	67.1	66.2	65.2	64.2
61	73.0	72.0	71.0	70.0	69.1	68.1	67.1	66.2	65.2	64.2
62	72.9	72.0	71.0	70.0	69.0	68.1	67.1	66.1	65.2	64.2
63	72.9	72.0	71.0	70.0	69.0	68.1	67.1	66.1	65.2	64.2
64	72.9	71.9	71.0	70.0	69.0	68.0	67.1	66.1	65.1	64.2
65	72.9	71.9	71.0	70.0	69.0	68.0	67.1	66.1	65.1	64.2
66	72.9	71.9	70.9	70.0	69.0	68.0	67.1	66.1	65.1	64.1
67	72.9	71.9	70.9	70.0	69.0	68.0	67.0	66.1	65.1	64.1
68	72.9	71.9	70.9	70.0	69.0	68.0	67.0	66.1	65.1	64.1
69	72.9	71.9	70.9	69.9	69.0	68.0	67.0	66.1	65.1	64.1
70	72.9	71.9	70.9	69.9	69.0	68.0	67.0	66.0	65.1	64.1
71	72.9	71.9	70.9	69.9	69.0	68.0	67.0	66.0	65.1	64.1
72	72.9	71.9	70.9	69.9	69.0	68.0	67.0	66.0	65.1	64.1

Ages	10	11	12	13	14	15	16	17	18	19
73	72.9	71.9	70.9	69.9	68.9	68.0	67.0	66.0	65.0	64.1
74	72.9	71.9	70.9	69.9	68.9	68.0	67.0	66.0	65.0	64.1
75	72.8	71.9	70.9	69.9	68.9	68.0	67.0	66.0	65.0	64.1
76	72.8	71.9	70.9	69.9	68.9	68.0	67.0	66.0	65.0	64.1
77	72.8	71.9	70.9	69.9	68.9	68.0	67.0	66.0	65.0	64.1
78	72.8	71.9	70.9	69.9	68.9	67.9	67.0	66.0	65.0	64.0
79	72.8	71.9	70.9	69.9	68.9	67.9	67.0	66.0	65.0	64.0
80	72.8	71.9	70.9	69.9	68.9	67.9	67.0	66.0	65.0	64.0
81	72.8	71.8	70.9	69.9	68.9	67.9	67.0	66.0	65.0	64.0
82	72.8	71.8	70.9	69.9	68.9	67.9	67.0	66.0	65.0	64.0
83	72.8	71.8	70.9	69.9	68.9	67.9	67.0	66.0	65.0	64.0
84	72.8	71.8	70.9	69.9	68.9	67.9	67.0	66.0	65.0	64.0
85	72.8	71.8	70.9	69.9	68.9	67.9	66.9	66.0	65.0	64.0
86	72.8	71.8	70.9	69.9	68.9	67.9	66.9	66.0	65.0	64.0
87	72.8	71.8	70.9	69.9	68.9	67.9	66.9	66.0	65.0	64.0
88	72.8	71.8	70.9	69.9	68.9	67.9	66.9	66.0	65.0	64.0
89	72.8	71.8	70.9	69.9	68.9	67.9	66.9	66.0	65.0	64.0
90	72.8	71.8	70.9	69.9	68.9	67.9	66.9	66.0	65.0	64.0
91	72.8	71.8	70.9	69.9	68.9	67.9	66.9	66.0	65.0	64.0
92	72.8	71.8	70.9	69.9	68.9	67.9	66.9	66.0	65.0	64.0
93	72.8	71.8	70.9	69.9	68.9	67.9	66.9	66.0	65.0	64.0

Ages	10	11	12	13	14	15	16	17	18	19
94	72.8	71.8	70.8	69.9	68.9	67.9	66.9	66.0	65.0	64.0
95	72.8	71.8	70.8	69.9	68.9	67.9	66.9	66.0	65.0	64.0
96	72.8	71.8	70.8	69.9	68.9	67.9	66.9	66.0	65.0	64.0
97	72.8	71.8	70.8	69.9	68.9	67.9	66.9	66.0	65.0	64.0
98	72.8	71.8	70.8	69.9	68.9	67.9	66.9	66.0	65.0	64.0
99	72.8	71.8	70.8	69.9	68.9	67.9	66.9	66.0	65.0	64.0
100	72.8	71.8	70.8	69.9	68.9	67.9	66.9	66.0	65.0	64.0
101	72.8	71.8	70.8	69.9	68.9	67.9	66.9	66.0	65.0	64.0
102	72.8	71.8	70.8	69.9	68.9	67.9	66.9	66.0	65.0	64.0
103	72.8	71.8	70.8	69.9	68.9	67.9	66.9	66.0	65.0	64.0
104	72.8	71.8	70.8	69.9	68.9	67.9	66.9	66.0	65.0	64.0
105	72.8	71.8	70.8	69.9	68.9	67.9	66.9	66.0	65.0	64.0
106	72.8	71.8	70.8	69.9	68.9	67.9	66.9	66.0	65.0	64.0
107	72.8	71.8	70.8	69.9	68.9	67.9	66.9	66.0	65.0	64.0
108	72.8	71.8	70.8	69.9	68.9	67.9	66.9	66.0	65.0	64.0
109	72.8	71.8	70.8	69.9	68.9	67.9	66.9	66.0	65.0	64.0
110	72.8	71.8	70.8	69.9	68.9	67.9	66.9	66.0	65.0	64.0
111	72.8	71.8	70.8	69.9	68.9	67.9	66.9	66.0	65.0	64.0
112	72.8	71.8	70.8	69.9	68.9	67.9	66.9	66.0	65.0	64.0
113	72.8	71.8	70.8	69.9	68.9	67.9	66.9	66.0	65.0	64.0
114	72.8	71.8	70.8	69.9	68.9	67.9	66.9	66.0	65.0	64.0

Ages	10	11	12	13	14	15	16	17	18	19
115+	72.8	71.8	70.8	69.9	68.9	67.9	66.9	66.0	65.0	64.0

Ages	20	21	22	23	24	25	26	27	28	29
20	70.1	69.6	69.1	68.7	68.3	67.9	67.5	67.2	66.9	66.6
21	69.6	69.1	68.6	68.2	67.7	67.3	66.9	66.6	66.2	65.9
22	69.1	68.6	68.1	67.6	67.2	66.7	66.3	65.9	65.6	65.2
23	68.7	68.2	67.6	67.1	66.6	66.2	65.7	65.3	64.9	64.6
24	68.3	67.7	67.2	66.6	66.1	65.6	65.2	64.7	64.3	63.9
25	67.9	67.3	66.7	66.2	65.6	65.1	64.6	64.2	63.7	63.3
26	67.5	66.9	66.3	65.7	65.2	64.6	64.1	63.6	63.2	62.8
27	67.2	66.6	65.9	65.3	64.7	64.2	63.6	63.1	62.7	62.2
28	66.9	66.2	65.6	64.9	64.3	63.7	63.2	62.7	62.1	61.7
29	66.6	65.9	65.2	64.6	63.9	63.3	62.8	62.2	61.7	61.2
30	66.3	65.6	64.9	64.2	63.6	62.9	62.3	61.8	61.2	60.7
31	66.1	65.3	64.6	63.9	63.2	62.6	62.0	61.4	60.8	60.2
32	65.8	65.1	64.3	63.6	62.9	62.2	61.6	61.0	60.4	59.8
33	65.6	64.8	64.1	63.3	62.6	61.9	61.3	60.6	60.0	59.4
34	65.4	64.6	63.8	63.1	62.3	61.6	60.9	60.3	59.6	59.0
35	65.2	64.4	63.6	62.8	62.1	61.4	60.6	59.9	59.3	58.6
36	65.0	64.2	63.4	62.6	61.9	61.1	60.4	59.6	59.0	58.3
37	64.9	64.0	63.2	62.4	61.6	60.9	60.1	59.4	58.7	58.0
38	64.7	63.9	63.0	62.2	61.4	60.6	59.9	59.1	58.4	57.7

Ages	20	21	22	23	24	25	26	27	28	29
39	64.6	63.7	62.9	62.1	61.2	60.4	59.6	58.9	58.1	57.4
40	64.4	63.6	62.7	61.9	61.1	60.2	59.4	58.7	57.9	57.1
41	64.3	63.5	62.6	61.7	60.9	60.1	59.3	58.5	57.7	56.9
42	64.2	63.3	62.5	61.6	60.8	59.9	59.1	58.3	57.5	56.7
43	64.1	63.2	62.4	61.5	60.6	59.8	58.9	58.1	57.3	56.5
44	64.0	63.1	62.2	61.4	60.5	59.6	58.8	57.9	57.1	56.3
45	64.0	63.0	62.2	61.3	60.4	59.5	58.6	57.8	56.9	56.1
46	63.9	63.0	62.1	61.2	60.3	59.4	58.5	57.7	56.8	56.0
47	63.8	62.9	62.0	61.1	60.2	59.3	58.4	57.5	56.7	55.8
48	63.7	62.8	61.9	61.0	60.1	59.2	58.3	57.4	56.5	55.7
49	63.7	62.8	61.8	60.9	60.0	59.1	58.2	57.3	56.4	55.6
50	63.6	62.7	61.8	60.8	59.9	59.0	58.1	57.2	56.3	55.4
51	63.6	62.6	61.7	60.8	59.9	58.9	58.0	57.1	56.2	55.3
52	63.5	62.6	61.7	60.7	59.8	58.9	58.0	57.1	56.1	55.2
53	63.5	62.5	61.6	60.7	59.7	58.8	57.9	57.0	56.1	55.2
54	63.5	62.5	61.6	60.6	59.7	58.8	57.8	56.9	56.0	55.1
55	63.4	62.5	61.5	60.6	59.6	58.7	57.8	56.8	55.9	55.0
56	63.4	62.4	61.5	60.5	59.6	58.7	57.7	56.8	55.9	54.9
57	63.4	62.4	61.5	60.5	59.6	58.6	57.7	56.7	55.8	54.9
58	63.3	62.4	61.4	60.5	59.5	58.6	57.6	56.7	55.8	54.8
59	63.3	62.3	61.4	60.4	59.5	58.5	57.6	56.7	55.7	54.8

Ages	20	21	22	23	24	25	26	27	28	29
60	63.3	62.3	61.4	60.4	59.5	58.5	57.6	56.6	55.7	54.7
61	63.3	62.3	61.3	60.4	59.4	58.5	57.5	56.6	55.6	54.7
62	63.2	62.3	61.3	60.4	59.4	58.4	57.5	56.5	55.6	54.7
63	63.2	62.3	61.3	60.3	59.4	58.4	57.5	56.5	55.6	54.6
64	63.2	62.2	61.3	60.3	59.4	58.4	57.4	56.5	55.5	54.6
65	63.2	62.2	61.3	60.3	59.3	58.4	57.4	56.5	55.5	54.6
66	63.2	62.2	61.2	60.3	59.3	58.4	57.4	56.4	55.5	54.5
67	63.2	62.2	61.2	60.3	59.3	58.3	57.4	56.4	55.5	54.5
68	63.1	62.2	61.2	60.2	59.3	58.3	57.4	56.4	55.4	54.5
69	63.1	62.2	61.2	60.2	59.3	58.3	57.3	56.4	55.4	54.5
70	63.1	62.2	61.2	60.2	59.3	58.3	57.3	56.4	55.4	54.4
71	63.1	62.1	61.2	60.2	59.2	58.3	57.3	56.4	55.4	54.4
72	63.1	62.1	61.2	60.2	59.2	58.3	57.3	56.3	55.4	54.4
73	63.1	62.1	61.2	60.2	59.2	58.3	57.3	56.3	55.4	54.4
74	63.1	62.1	61.2	60.2	59.2	58.2	57.3	56.3	55.4	54.4
75	63.1	62.1	61.1	60.2	59.2	58.2	57.3	56.3	55.3	54.4
76	63.1	62.1	61.1	60.2	59.2	58.2	57.3	56.3	55.3	54.4
77	63.1	62.1	61.1	60.2	59.2	58.2	57.3	56.3	55.3	54.4
78	63.1	62.1	61.1	60.2	59.2	58.2	57.3	56.3	55.3	54.4
79	63.1	62.1	61.1	60.2	59.2	58.2	57.2	56.3	55.3	54.3
80	63.1	62.1	61.1	60.1	59.2	58.2	57.2	56.3	55.3	54.3

Ages	20	21	22	23	24	25	26	27	28	29
81	63.1	62.1	61.1	60.1	59.2	58.2	57.2	56.3	55.3	54.3
82	63.1	62.1	61.1	60.1	59.2	58.2	57.2	56.3	55.3	54.3
83	63.1	62.1	61.1	60.1	59.2	58.2	57.2	56.3	55.3	54.3
84	63.0	62.1	61.1	60.1	59.2	58.2	57.2	56.3	55.3	54.3
85	63.0	62.1	61.1	60.1	59.2	58.2	57.2	56.3	55.3	54.3
86	63.0	62.1	61.1	60.1	59.2	58.2	57.2	56.2	55.3	54.3
87	63.0	62.1	61.1	60.1	59.2	58.2	57.2	56.2	55.3	54.3
88	63.0	62.1	61.1	60.1	59.2	58.2	57.2	56.2	55.3	54.3
89	63.0	62.1	61.1	60.1	59.1	58.2	57.2	56.2	55.3	54.3
90	63.0	62.1	61.1	60.1	59.1	58.2	57.2	56.2	55.3	54.3
91	63.0	62.1	61.1	60.1	59.1	58.2	57.2	56.2	55.3	54.3
92	63.0	62.1	61.1	60.1	59.1	58.2	57.2	56.2	55.3	54.3
93	63.0	62.1	61.1	60.1	59.1	58.2	57.2	56.2	55.3	54.3
94	63.0	62.1	61.1	60.1	59.1	58.2	57.2	56.2	55.3	54.3
95	63.0	62.1	61.1	60.1	59.1	58.2	57.2	56.2	55.3	54.3
96	63.0	62.1	61.1	60.1	59.1	58.2	57.2	56.2	55.3	54.3
97	63.0	62.1	61.1	60.1	59.1	58.2	57.2	56.2	55.3	54.3
98	63.0	62.1	61.1	60.1	59.1	58.2	57.2	56.2	55.3	54.3
99	63.0	62.1	61.1	60.1	59.1	58.2	57.2	56.2	55.3	54.3
100	63.0	62.1	61.1	60.1	59.1	58.2	57.2	56.2	55.3	54.3
101	63.0	62.1	61.1	60.1	59.1	58.2	57.2	56.2	55.3	54.3

Ages	20	21	22	23	24	25	26	27	28	29
102	63.0	62.1	61.1	60.1	59.1	58.2	57.2	56.2	55.3	54.3
103	63.0	62.1	61.1	60.1	59.1	58.2	57.2	56.2	55.3	54.3
104	63.0	62.1	61.1	60.1	59.1	58.2	57.2	56.2	55.3	54.3
105	63.0	62.1	61.1	60.1	59.1	58.2	57.2	56.2	55.3	54.3
106	63.0	62.1	61.1	60.1	59.1	58.2	57.2	56.2	55.3	54.3
107	63.0	62.1	61.1	60.1	59.1	58.2	57.2	56.2	55.3	54.3
108	63.0	62.1	61.1	60.1	59.1	58.2	57.2	56.2	55.3	54.3
109	63.0	62.1	61.1	60.1	59.1	58.2	57.2	56.2	55.3	54.3
110	63.0	62.1	61.1	60.1	59.1	58.2	57.2	56.2	55.3	54.3
111	63.0	62.1	61.1	60.1	59.1	58.2	57.2	56.2	55.3	54.3
112	63.0	62.1	61.1	60.1	59.1	58.2	57.2	56.2	55.3	54.3
113	63.0	62.1	61.1	60.1	59.1	58.2	57.2	56.2	55.3	54.3
114	63.0	62.1	61.1	60.1	59.1	58.2	57.2	56.2	55.3	54.3
115+	63.0	62.1	61.1	60.1	59.1	58.2	57.2	56.2	55.3	54.3

Ages	30	31	32	33	34	35	36	37	38	39
30	60.2	59.7	59.2	58.8	58.4	58.0	57.6	57.3	57.0	56.7
31	59.7	59.2	58.7	58.2	57.8	57.4	57.0	56.6	56.3	56.0
32	59.2	58.7	58.2	57.7	57.2	56.8	56.4	56.0	55.6	55.3
33	58.8	58.2	57.7	57.2	56.7	56.2	55.8	55.4	55.0	54.7
34	58.4	57.8	57.2	56.7	56.2	55.7	55.3	54.8	54.4	54.0
35	58.0	57.4	56.8	56.2	55.7	55.2	54.7	54.3	53.8	53.4

Ages	30	31	32	33	34	35	36	37	38	39
36	57.6	57.0	56.4	55.8	55.3	54.7	54.2	53.7	53.3	52.8
37	57.3	56.6	56.0	55.4	54.8	54.3	53.7	53.2	52.7	52.3
38	57.0	56.3	55.6	55.0	54.4	53.8	53.3	52.7	52.2	51.7
39	56.7	56.0	55.3	54.7	54.0	53.4	52.8	52.3	51.7	51.2
40	56.4	55.7	55.0	54.3	53.7	53.0	52.4	51.8	51.3	50.8
41	56.1	55.4	54.7	54.0	53.3	52.7	52.0	51.4	50.9	50.3
42	55.9	55.2	54.4	53.7	53.0	52.3	51.7	51.1	50.4	49.9
43	55.7	54.9	54.2	53.4	52.7	52.0	51.3	50.7	50.1	49.5
44	55.5	54.7	53.9	53.2	52.4	51.7	51.0	50.4	49.7	49.1
45	55.3	54.5	53.7	52.9	52.2	51.5	50.7	50.0	49.4	48.7
46	55.1	54.3	53.5	52.7	52.0	51.2	50.5	49.8	49.1	48.4
47	55.0	54.1	53.3	52.5	51.7	51.0	50.2	49.5	48.8	48.1
48	54.8	54.0	53.2	52.3	51.5	50.8	50.0	49.2	48.5	47.8
49	54.7	53.8	53.0	52.2	51.4	50.6	49.8	49.0	48.2	47.5
50	54.6	53.7	52.9	52.0	51.2	50.4	49.6	48.8	48.0	47.3
51	54.5	53.6	52.7	51.9	51.0	50.2	49.4	48.6	47.8	47.0
52	54.4	53.5	52.6	51.7	50.9	50.0	49.2	48.4	47.6	46.8
53	54.3	53.4	52.5	51.6	50.8	49.9	49.1	48.2	47.4	46.6
54	54.2	53.3	52.4	51.5	50.6	49.8	48.9	48.1	47.2	46.4
55	54.1	53.2	52.3	51.4	50.5	49.7	48.8	47.9	47.1	46.3
56	54.0	53.1	52.2	51.3	50.4	49.5	48.7	47.8	47.0	46.1

Ages	30	31	32	33	34	35	36	37	38	39
57	54.0	53.0	52.1	51.2	50.3	49.4	48.6	47.7	46.8	46.0
58	53.9	53.0	52.1	51.2	50.3	49.4	48.5	47.6	46.7	45.8
59	53.8	52.9	52.0	51.1	50.2	49.3	48.4	47.5	46.6	45.7
60	53.8	52.9	51.9	51.0	50.1	49.2	48.3	47.4	46.5	45.6
61	53.8	52.8	51.9	51.0	50.0	49.1	48.2	47.3	46.4	45.5
62	53.7	52.8	51.8	50.9	50.0	49.1	48.1	47.2	46.3	45.4
63	53.7	52.7	51.8	50.9	49.9	49.0	48.1	47.2	46.3	45.3
64	53.6	52.7	51.8	50.8	49.9	48.9	48.0	47.1	46.2	45.3
65	53.6	52.7	51.7	50.8	49.8	48.9	48.0	47.0	46.1	45.2
66	53.6	52.6	51.7	50.7	49.8	48.9	47.9	47.0	46.1	45.1
67	53.6	52.6	51.7	50.7	49.8	48.8	47.9	46.9	46.0	45.1
68	53.5	52.6	51.6	50.7	49.7	48.8	47.8	46.9	46.0	45.0
69	53.5	52.6	51.6	50.6	49.7	48.7	47.8	46.9	45.9	45.0
70	53.5	52.5	51.6	50.6	49.7	48.7	47.8	46.8	45.9	44.9
71	53.5	52.5	51.6	50.6	49.6	48.7	47.7	46.8	45.9	44.9
72	53.5	52.5	51.5	50.6	49.6	48.7	47.7	46.8	45.8	44.9
73	53.4	52.5	51.5	50.6	49.6	48.6	47.7	46.7	45.8	44.8
74	53.4	52.5	51.5	50.5	49.6	48.6	47.7	46.7	45.8	44.8
75	53.4	52.5	51.5	50.5	49.6	48.6	47.7	46.7	45.7	44.8
76	53.4	52.4	51.5	50.5	49.6	48.6	47.6	46.7	45.7	44.8
77	53.4	52.4	51.5	50.5	49.5	48.6	47.6	46.7	45.7	44.8

Ages	30	31	32	33	34	35	36	37	38	39
78	53.4	52.4	51.5	50.5	49.5	48.6	47.6	46.6	45.7	44.7
79	53.4	52.4	51.5	50.5	49.5	48.6	47.6	46.6	45.7	44.7
80	53.4	52.4	51.4	50.5	49.5	48.5	47.6	46.6	45.7	44.7
81	53.4	52.4	51.4	50.5	49.5	48.5	47.6	46.6	45.7	44.7
82	53.4	52.4	51.4	50.5	49.5	48.5	47.6	46.6	45.6	44.7
83	53.4	52.4	51.4	50.5	49.5	48.5	47.6	46.6	45.6	44.7
84	53.4	52.4	51.4	50.5	49.5	48.5	47.6	46.6	45.6	44.7
85	53.3	52.4	51.4	50.4	49.5	48.5	47.5	46.6	45.6	44.7
86	53.3	52.4	51.4	50.4	49.5	48.5	47.5	46.6	45.6	44.6
87	53.3	52.4	51.4	50.4	49.5	48.5	47.5	46.6	45.6	44.6
88	53.3	52.4	51.4	50.4	49.5	48.5	47.5	46.6	45.6	44.6
89	53.3	52.4	51.4	50.4	49.5	48.5	47.5	46.6	45.6	44.6
90	53.3	52.4	51.4	50.4	49.5	48.5	47.5	46.6	45.6	44.6
91	53.3	52.4	51.4	50.4	49.5	48.5	47.5	46.6	45.6	44.6
92	53.3	52.4	51.4	50.4	49.5	48.5	47.5	46.6	45.6	44.6
93	53.3	52.4	51.4	50.4	49.5	48.5	47.5	46.6	45.6	44.6
94	53.3	52.4	51.4	50.4	49.5	48.5	47.5	46.6	45.6	44.6
95	53.3	52.4	51.4	50.4	49.5	48.5	47.5	46.5	45.6	44.6
96	53.3	52.4	51.4	50.4	49.5	48.5	47.5	46.5	45.6	44.6
97	53.3	52.4	51.4	50.4	49.5	48.5	47.5	46.5	45.6	44.6
98	53.3	52.4	51.4	50.4	49.5	48.5	47.5	46.5	45.6	44.6

Ages	30	31	32	33	34	35	36	37	38	39
99	53.3	52.4	51.4	50.4	49.5	48.5	47.5	46.5	45.6	44.6
100	53.3	52.4	51.4	50.4	49.5	48.5	47.5	46.5	45.6	44.6
101	53.3	52.4	51.4	50.4	49.5	48.5	47.5	46.5	45.6	44.6
102	53.3	52.4	51.4	50.4	49.5	48.5	47.5	46.5	45.6	44.6
103	53.3	52.4	51.4	50.4	49.5	48.5	47.5	46.5	45.6	44.6
104	53.3	52.4	51.4	50.4	49.5	48.5	47.5	46.5	45.6	44.6
105	53.3	52.4	51.4	50.4	49.4	48.5	47.5	46.5	45.6	44.6
106	53.3	52.4	51.4	50.4	49.4	48.5	47.5	46.5	45.6	44.6
107	53.3	52.4	51.4	50.4	49.4	48.5	47.5	46.5	45.6	44.6
108	53.3	52.4	51.4	50.4	49.4	48.5	47.5	46.5	45.6	44.6
109	53.3	52.4	51.4	50.4	49.4	48.5	47.5	46.5	45.6	44.6
110	53.3	52.4	51.4	50.4	49.4	48.5	47.5	46.5	45.6	44.6
111	53.3	52.4	51.4	50.4	49.4	48.5	47.5	46.5	45.6	44.6
112	53.3	52.4	51.4	50.4	49.4	48.5	47.5	46.5	45.6	44.6
113	53.3	52.4	51.4	50.4	49.4	48.5	47.5	46.5	45.6	44.6
114	53.3	52.4	51.4	50.4	49.4	48.5	47.5	46.5	45.6	44.6
115+	53.3	52.4	51.4	50.4	49.4	48.5	47.5	46.5	45.6	44.6
Ages	40	41	42	43	44	45	46	47	48	49
40	50.2	49.8	49.3	48.9	48.5	48.1	47.7	47.4	47.1	46.8
41		49.8	49.3	48.8	48.3	47.9	47.5	47.1	46.7	46.4	46.1
42			49.3	48.8	48.3	47.8	47.3	46.9	46.5	46.1	45.8	45.4

Ages	40	41	42	43	44	45	46	47	48	49
43	48.9	48.3	47.8	47.3	46.8	46.3	45.9	45.5	45.1	44.8
44	48.5	47.9	47.3	46.8	46.3	45.8	45.4	44.9	44.5	44.2
45	48.1	47.5	46.9	46.3	45.8	45.3	44.8	44.4	44.0	43.6
46	47.7	47.1	46.5	45.9	45.4	44.8	44.3	43.9	43.4	43.0
47	47.4	46.7	46.1	45.5	44.9	44.4	43.9	43.4	42.9	42.4
48	47.1	46.4	45.8	45.1	44.5	44.0	43.4	42.9	42.4	41.9
49	46.8	46.1	45.4	44.8	44.2	43.6	43.0	42.4	41.9	41.4
50	46.5	45.8	45.1	44.4	43.8	43.2	42.6	42.0	41.5	40.9
51	46.3	45.5	44.8	44.1	43.5	42.8	42.2	41.6	41.0	40.5
52	46.0	45.3	44.6	43.8	43.2	42.5	41.8	41.2	40.6	40.1
53	45.8	45.1	44.3	43.6	42.9	42.2	41.5	40.9	40.3	39.7
54	45.6	44.8	44.1	43.3	42.6	41.9	41.2	40.5	39.9	39.3
55	45.5	44.7	43.9	43.1	42.4	41.6	40.9	40.2	39.6	38.9
56	45.3	44.5	43.7	42.9	42.1	41.4	40.7	40.0	39.3	38.6
57	45.1	44.3	43.5	42.7	41.9	41.2	40.4	39.7	39.0	38.3
58	45.0	44.2	43.3	42.5	41.7	40.9	40.2	39.4	38.7	38.0
59	44.9	44.0	43.2	42.4	41.5	40.7	40.0	39.2	38.5	37.8
60	44.7	43.9	43.0	42.2	41.4	40.6	39.8	39.0	38.2	37.5
61	44.6	43.8	42.9	42.1	41.2	40.4	39.6	38.8	38.0	37.3
62	44.5	43.7	42.8	41.9	41.1	40.3	39.4	38.6	37.8	37.1
63	44.5	43.6	42.7	41.8	41.0	40.1	39.3	38.5	37.7	36.9

Ages	40	41	42	43	44	45	46	47	48	49
64	44.4	43.5	42.6	41.7	40.8	40.0	39.2	38.3	37.5	36.7
65	44.3	43.4	42.5	41.6	40.7	39.9	39.0	38.2	37.4	36.6
66	44.2	43.3	42.4	41.5	40.6	39.8	38.9	38.1	37.2	36.4
67	44.2	43.3	42.3	41.4	40.6	39.7	38.8	38.0	37.1	36.3
68	44.1	43.2	42.3	41.4	40.5	39.6	38.7	37.9	37.0	36.2
69	44.1	43.1	42.2	41.3	40.4	39.5	38.6	37.8	36.9	36.0
70	44.0	43.1	42.2	41.3	40.3	39.4	38.6	37.7	36.8	35.9
71	44.0	43.0	42.1	41.2	40.3	39.4	38.5	37.6	36.7	35.9
72	43.9	43.0	42.1	41.1	40.2	39.3	38.4	37.5	36.6	35.8
73	43.9	43.0	42.0	41.1	40.2	39.3	38.4	37.5	36.6	35.7
74	43.9	42.9	42.0	41.1	40.1	39.2	38.3	37.4	36.5	35.6
75	43.8	42.9	42.0	41.0	40.1	39.2	38.3	37.4	36.5	35.6
76	43.8	42.9	41.9	41.0	40.1	39.1	38.2	37.3	36.4	35.5
77	43.8	42.9	41.9	41.0	40.0	39.1	38.2	37.3	36.4	35.5
78	43.8	42.8	41.9	40.9	40.0	39.1	38.2	37.2	36.3	35.4
79	43.8	42.8	41.9	40.9	40.0	39.1	38.1	37.2	36.3	35.4
80	43.7	42.8	41.8	40.9	40.0	39.0	38.1	37.2	36.3	35.4
81	43.7	42.8	41.8	40.9	39.9	39.0	38.1	37.2	36.2	35.3
82	43.7	42.8	41.8	40.9	39.9	39.0	38.1	37.1	36.2	35.3
83	43.7	42.8	41.8	40.9	39.9	39.0	38.0	37.1	36.2	35.3
84	43.7	42.7	41.8	40.8	39.9	39.0	38.0	37.1	36.2	35.3

Ages	40	41	42	43	44	45	46	47	48	49
85	43.7	42.7	41.8	40.8	39.9	38.9	38.0	37.1	36.2	35.2
86	43.7	42.7	41.8	40.8	39.9	38.9	38.0	37.1	36.1	35.2
87	43.7	42.7	41.8	40.8	39.9	38.9	38.0	37.0	36.1	35.2
88	43.7	42.7	41.8	40.8	39.9	38.9	38.0	37.0	36.1	35.2
89	43.7	42.7	41.7	40.8	39.8	38.9	38.0	37.0	36.1	35.2
90	43.7	42.7	41.7	40.8	39.8	38.9	38.0	37.0	36.1	35.2
91	43.7	42.7	41.7	40.8	39.8	38.9	37.9	37.0	36.1	35.2
92	43.7	42.7	41.7	40.8	39.8	38.9	37.9	37.0	36.1	35.1
93	43.7	42.7	41.7	40.8	39.8	38.9	37.9	37.0	36.1	35.1
94	43.7	42.7	41.7	40.8	39.8	38.9	37.9	37.0	36.1	35.1
95	43.6	42.7	41.7	40.8	39.8	38.9	37.9	37.0	36.1	35.1
96	43.6	42.7	41.7	40.8	39.8	38.9	37.9	37.0	36.1	35.1
97	43.6	42.7	41.7	40.8	39.8	38.9	37.9	37.0	36.1	35.1
98	43.6	42.7	41.7	40.8	39.8	38.9	37.9	37.0	36.0	35.1
99	43.6	42.7	41.7	40.8	39.8	38.9	37.9	37.0	36.0	35.1
100	43.6	42.7	41.7	40.8	39.8	38.9	37.9	37.0	36.0	35.1
101	43.6	42.7	41.7	40.8	39.8	38.9	37.9	37.0	36.0	35.1
102	43.6	42.7	41.7	40.8	39.8	38.9	37.9	37.0	36.0	35.1
103	43.6	42.7	41.7	40.8	39.8	38.9	37.9	37.0	36.0	35.1
104	43.6	42.7	41.7	40.8	39.8	38.8	37.9	37.0	36.0	35.1
105	43.6	42.7	41.7	40.8	39.8	38.8	37.9	37.0	36.0	35.1

Ages	40	41	42	43	44	45	46	47	48	49
106	43.6	42.7	41.7	40.8	39.8	38.8	37.9	37.0	36.0	35.1
107	43.6	42.7	41.7	40.8	39.8	38.8	37.9	37.0	36.0	35.1
108	43.6	42.7	41.7	40.8	39.8	38.8	37.9	37.0	36.0	35.1
109	43.6	42.7	41.7	40.7	39.8	38.8	37.9	37.0	36.0	35.1
110	43.6	42.7	41.7	40.7	39.8	38.8	37.9	37.0	36.0	35.1
111	43.6	42.7	41.7	40.7	39.8	38.8	37.9	37.0	36.0	35.1
112	43.6	42.7	41.7	40.7	39.8	38.8	37.9	37.0	36.0	35.1
113	43.6	42.7	41.7	40.7	39.8	38.8	37.9	37.0	36.0	35.1
114	43.6	42.7	41.7	40.7	39.8	38.8	37.9	37.0	36.0	35.1
115+	43.6	42.7	41.7	40.7	39.8	38.8	37.9	37.0	36.0	35.1

Ages	50	51	52	53	54	55	56	57	58	59
50	40.4	40.0	39.5	39.1	38.7	38.3	38.0	37.6	37.3	37.1
51	40.0	39.5	39.0	38.5	38.1	37.7	37.4	37.0	36.7	36.4
52	39.5	39.0	38.5	38.0	37.6	37.2	36.8	36.4	36.0	35.7
53	39.1	38.5	38.0	37.5	37.1	36.6	36.2	35.8	35.4	35.1
54	38.7	38.1	37.6	37.1	36.6	36.1	35.7	35.2	34.8	34.5
55	38.3	37.7	37.2	36.6	36.1	35.6	35.1	34.7	34.3	33.9
56	38.0	37.4	36.8	36.2	35.7	35.1	34.7	34.2	33.7	33.3
57	37.6	37.0	36.4	35.8	35.2	34.7	34.2	33.7	33.2	32.8
58	37.3	36.7	36.0	35.4	34.8	34.3	33.7	33.2	32.8	32.3
59	37.1	36.4	35.7	35.1	34.5	33.9	33.3	32.8	32.3	31.8

Ages	50	51	52	53	54	55	56	57	58	59
60	36.8	36.1	35.4	34.8	34.1	33.5	32.9	32.4	31.9	31.3
61	36.6	35.8	35.1	34.5	33.8	33.2	32.6	32.0	31.4	30.9
62	36.3	35.6	34.9	34.2	33.5	32.9	32.2	31.6	31.1	30.5
63	36.1	35.4	34.6	33.9	33.2	32.6	31.9	31.3	30.7	30.1
64	35.9	35.2	34.4	33.7	33.0	32.3	31.6	31.0	30.4	29.8
65	35.8	35.0	34.2	33.5	32.7	32.0	31.4	30.7	30.0	29.4
66	35.6	34.8	34.0	33.3	32.5	31.8	31.1	30.4	29.8	29.1
67	35.5	34.7	33.9	33.1	32.3	31.6	30.9	30.2	29.5	28.8
68	35.3	34.5	33.7	32.9	32.1	31.4	30.7	29.9	29.2	28.6
69	35.2	34.4	33.6	32.8	32.0	31.2	30.5	29.7	29.0	28.3
70	35.1	34.3	33.4	32.6	31.8	31.1	30.3	29.5	28.8	28.1
71	35.0	34.2	33.3	32.5	31.7	30.9	30.1	29.4	28.6	27.9
72	34.9	34.1	33.2	32.4	31.6	30.8	30.0	29.2	28.4	27.7
73	34.8	34.0	33.1	32.3	31.5	30.6	29.8	29.1	28.3	27.5
74	34.8	33.9	33.0	32.2	31.4	30.5	29.7	28.9	28.1	27.4
75	34.7	33.8	33.0	32.1	31.3	30.4	29.6	28.8	28.0	27.2
76	34.6	33.8	32.9	32.0	31.2	30.3	29.5	28.7	27.9	27.1
77	34.6	33.7	32.8	32.0	31.1	30.3	29.4	28.6	27.8	27.0
78	34.5	33.6	32.8	31.9	31.0	30.2	29.3	28.5	27.7	26.9
79	34.5	33.6	32.7	31.8	31.0	30.1	29.3	28.4	27.6	26.8
80	34.5	33.6	32.7	31.8	30.9	30.1	29.2	28.4	27.5	26.7

Ages	50	51	52	53	54	55	56	57	58	59
81	34.4	33.5	32.6	31.8	30.9	30.0	29.2	28.3	27.5	26.6
82	34.4	33.5	32.6	31.7	30.8	30.0	29.1	28.3	27.4	26.6
83	34.4	33.5	32.6	31.7	30.8	29.9	29.1	28.2	27.4	26.5
84	34.3	33.4	32.5	31.7	30.8	29.9	29.0	28.2	27.3	26.5
85	34.3	33.4	32.5	31.6	30.7	29.9	29.0	28.1	27.3	26.4
86	34.3	33.4	32.5	31.6	30.7	29.8	29.0	28.1	27.2	26.4
87	34.3	33.4	32.5	31.6	30.7	29.8	28.9	28.1	27.2	26.4
88	34.3	33.4	32.5	31.6	30.7	29.8	28.9	28.0	27.2	26.3
89	34.3	33.3	32.4	31.5	30.7	29.8	28.9	28.0	27.2	26.3
90	34.2	33.3	32.4	31.5	30.6	29.8	28.9	28.0	27.1	26.3
91	34.2	33.3	32.4	31.5	30.6	29.7	28.9	28.0	27.1	26.3
92	34.2	33.3	32.4	31.5	30.6	29.7	28.8	28.0	27.1	26.2
93	34.2	33.3	32.4	31.5	30.6	29.7	28.8	28.0	27.1	26.2
94	34.2	33.3	32.4	31.5	30.6	29.7	28.8	27.9	27.1	26.2
95	34.2	33.3	32.4	31.5	30.6	29.7	28.8	27.9	27.1	26.2
96	34.2	33.3	32.4	31.5	30.6	29.7	28.8	27.9	27.0	26.2
97	34.2	33.3	32.4	31.5	30.6	29.7	28.8	27.9	27.0	26.2
98	34.2	33.3	32.4	31.5	30.6	29.7	28.8	27.9	27.0	26.2
99	34.2	33.3	32.4	31.5	30.6	29.7	28.8	27.9	27.0	26.2
100	34.2	33.3	32.4	31.5	30.6	29.7	28.8	27.9	27.0	26.1
101	34.2	33.3	32.4	31.5	30.6	29.7	28.8	27.9	27.0	26.1

Ages	50	51	52	53	54	55	56	57	58	59
102	34.2	33.3	32.4	31.4	30.5	29.7	28.8	27.9	27.0	26.1
103	34.2	33.3	32.4	31.4	30.5	29.7	28.8	27.9	27.0	26.1
104	34.2	33.3	32.4	31.4	30.5	29.6	28.8	27.9	27.0	26.1
105	34.2	33.3	32.3	31.4	30.5	29.6	28.8	27.9	27.0	26.1
106	34.2	33.3	32.3	31.4	30.5	29.6	28.8	27.9	27.0	26.1
107	34.2	33.3	32.3	31.4	30.5	29.6	28.8	27.9	27.0	26.1
108	34.2	33.3	32.3	31.4	30.5	29.6	28.8	27.9	27.0	26.1
109	34.2	33.3	32.3	31.4	30.5	29.6	28.7	27.9	27.0	26.1
110	34.2	33.3	32.3	31.4	30.5	29.6	28.7	27.9	27.0	26.1
111	34.2	33.3	32.3	31.4	30.5	29.6	28.7	27.9	27.0	26.1
112	34.2	33.3	32.3	31.4	30.5	29.6	28.7	27.9	27.0	26.1
113	34.2	33.3	32.3	31.4	30.5	29.6	28.7	27.9	27.0	26.1
114	34.2	33.3	32.3	31.4	30.5	29.6	28.7	27.9	27.0	26.1
115+	34.2	33.3	32.3	31.4	30.5	29.6	28.7	27.9	27.0	26.1

Ages	60	61	62	63	64	65	66	67	68	69
60	30.9	30.4	30.0	29.6	29.2	28.8	28.5	28.2	27.9	27.6
61	30.4	29.9	29.5	29.0	28.6	28.3	27.9	27.6	27.3	27.0
62	30.0	29.5	29.0	28.5	28.1	27.7	27.3	27.0	26.7	26.4
63	29.6	29.0	28.5	28.1	27.6	27.2	26.8	26.4	26.1	25.7
64	29.2	28.6	28.1	27.6	27.1	26.7	26.3	25.9	25.5	25.2
65	28.8	28.3	27.7	27.2	26.7	26.2	25.8	25.4	25.0	24.6

Ages	60	61	62	63	64	65	66	67	68	69
66	28.5	27.9	27.3	26.8	26.3	25.8	25.3	24.9	24.5	24.1
67	28.2	27.6	27.0	26.4	25.9	25.4	24.9	24.4	24.0	23.6
68	27.9	27.3	26.7	26.1	25.5	25.0	24.5	24.0	23.5	23.1
69	27.6	27.0	26.4	25.7	25.2	24.6	24.1	23.6	23.1	22.6
70	27.4	26.7	26.1	25.4	24.8	24.3	23.7	23.2	22.7	22.2
71	27.2	26.5	25.8	25.2	24.5	23.9	23.4	22.8	22.3	21.8
72	27.0	26.3	25.6	24.9	24.3	23.7	23.1	22.5	22.0	21.4
73	26.8	26.1	25.4	24.7	24.0	23.4	22.8	22.2	21.6	21.1
74	26.6	25.9	25.2	24.5	23.8	23.1	22.5	21.9	21.3	20.8
75	26.5	25.7	25.0	24.3	23.6	22.9	22.3	21.6	21.0	20.5
76	26.3	25.6	24.8	24.1	23.4	22.7	22.0	21.4	20.8	20.2
77	26.2	25.4	24.7	23.9	23.2	22.5	21.8	21.2	20.6	19.9
78	26.1	25.3	24.6	23.8	23.1	22.4	21.7	21.0	20.3	19.7
79	26.0	25.2	24.4	23.7	22.9	22.2	21.5	20.8	20.1	19.5
80	25.9	25.1	24.3	23.6	22.8	22.1	21.3	20.6	20.0	19.3
81	25.8	25.0	24.2	23.4	22.7	21.9	21.2	20.5	19.8	19.1
82	25.8	24.9	24.1	23.4	22.6	21.8	21.1	20.4	19.7	19.0
83	25.7	24.9	24.1	23.3	22.5	21.7	21.0	20.2	19.5	18.8
84	25.6	24.8	24.0	23.2	22.4	21.6	20.9	20.1	19.4	18.7
85	25.6	24.8	23.9	23.1	22.3	21.6	20.8	20.1	19.3	18.6
86	25.5	24.7	23.9	23.1	22.3	21.5	20.7	20.0	19.2	18.5

Ages	60	61	62	63	64	65	66	67	68	69
87	25.5	24.7	23.8	23.0	22.2	21.4	20.7	19.9	19.2	18.4
88	25.5	24.6	23.8	23.0	22.2	21.4	20.6	19.8	19.1	18.3
89	25.4	24.6	23.8	22.9	22.1	21.3	20.5	19.8	19.0	18.3
90	25.4	24.6	23.7	22.9	22.1	21.3	20.5	19.7	19.0	18.2
91	25.4	24.5	23.7	22.9	22.1	21.3	20.5	19.7	18.9	18.2
92	25.4	24.5	23.7	22.9	22.0	21.2	20.4	19.6	18.9	18.1
93	25.4	24.5	23.7	22.8	22.0	21.2	20.4	19.6	18.8	18.1
94	25.3	24.5	23.6	22.8	22.0	21.2	20.4	19.6	18.8	18.0
95	25.3	24.5	23.6	22.8	22.0	21.1	20.3	19.6	18.8	18.0
96	25.3	24.5	23.6	22.8	21.9	21.1	20.3	19.5	18.8	18.0
97	25.3	24.5	23.6	22.8	21.9	21.1	20.3	19.5	18.7	18.0
98	25.3	24.4	23.6	22.8	21.9	21.1	20.3	19.5	18.7	17.9
99	25.3	24.4	23.6	22.7	21.9	21.1	20.3	19.5	18.7	17.9
100	25.3	24.4	23.6	22.7	21.9	21.1	20.3	19.5	18.7	17.9
101	25.3	24.4	23.6	22.7	21.9	21.1	20.2	19.4	18.7	17.9
102	25.3	24.4	23.6	22.7	21.9	21.1	20.2	19.4	18.6	17.9
103	25.3	24.4	23.6	22.7	21.9	21.0	20.2	19.4	18.6	17.9
104	25.3	24.4	23.5	22.7	21.9	21.0	20.2	19.4	18.6	17.8
105	25.3	24.4	23.5	22.7	21.9	21.0	20.2	19.4	18.6	17.8
106	25.3	24.4	23.5	22.7	21.9	21.0	20.2	19.4	18.6	17.8
107	25.2	24.4	23.5	22.7	21.8	21.0	20.2	19.4	18.6	17.8

Ages	60	61	62	63	64	65	66	67	68	69
108	25.2	24.4	23.5	22.7	21.8	21.0	20.2	19.4	18.6	17.8
109	25.2	24.4	23.5	22.7	21.8	21.0	20.2	19.4	18.6	17.8
110	25.2	24.4	23.5	22.7	21.8	21.0	20.2	19.4	18.6	17.8
111	25.2	24.4	23.5	22.7	21.8	21.0	20.2	19.4	18.6	17.8
112	25.2	24.4	23.5	22.7	21.8	21.0	20.2	19.4	18.6	17.8
113	25.2	24.4	23.5	22.7	21.8	21.0	20.2	19.4	18.6	17.8
114	25.2	24.4	23.5	22.7	21.8	21.0	20.2	19.4	18.6	17.8
115+	25.2	24.4	23.5	22.7	21.8	21.0	20.2	19.4	18.6	17.8

Ages	70	71	72	73	74	75	76	77	78	79
70	21.8	21.3	20.9	20.6	20.2	19.9	19.6	19.4	19.1	18.9
71	21.3	20.9	20.5	20.1	19.7	19.4	19.1	18.8	18.5	18.3
72	20.9	20.5	20.0	19.6	19.3	18.9	18.6	18.3	18.0	17.7
73	20.6	20.1	19.6	19.2	18.8	18.4	18.1	17.8	17.5	17.2
74	20.2	19.7	19.3	18.8	18.4	18.0	17.6	17.3	17.0	16.7
75	19.9	19.4	18.9	18.4	18.0	17.6	17.2	16.8	16.5	16.2
76	19.6	19.1	18.6	18.1	17.6	17.2	16.8	16.4	16.0	15.7
77	19.4	18.8	18.3	17.8	17.3	16.8	16.4	16.0	15.6	15.3
78	19.1	18.5	18.0	17.5	17.0	16.5	16.0	15.6	15.2	14.9
79	18.9	18.3	17.7	17.2	16.7	16.2	15.7	15.3	14.9	14.5
80	18.7	18.1	17.5	16.9	16.4	15.9	15.4	15.0	14.5	14.1
81	18.5	17.9	17.3	16.7	16.2	15.6	15.1	14.7	14.2	13.8

Ages	70	71	72	73	74	75	76	77	78	79
82	18.3	17.7	17.1	16.5	15.9	15.4	14.9	14.4	13.9	13.5
83	18.2	17.5	16.9	16.3	15.7	15.2	14.7	14.2	13.7	13.2
84	18.0	17.4	16.7	16.1	15.5	15.0	14.4	13.9	13.4	13.0
85	17.9	17.3	16.6	16.0	15.4	14.8	14.3	13.7	13.2	12.8
86	17.8	17.1	16.5	15.8	15.2	14.6	14.1	13.5	13.0	12.5
87	17.7	17.0	16.4	15.7	15.1	14.5	13.9	13.4	12.9	12.4
88	17.6	16.9	16.3	15.6	15.0	14.4	13.8	13.2	12.7	12.2
89	17.6	16.9	16.2	15.5	14.9	14.3	13.7	13.1	12.6	12.0
90	17.5	16.8	16.1	15.4	14.8	14.2	13.6	13.0	12.4	11.9
91	17.4	16.7	16.0	15.4	14.7	14.1	13.5	12.9	12.3	11.8
92	17.4	16.7	16.0	15.3	14.6	14.0	13.4	12.8	12.2	11.7
93	17.3	16.6	15.9	15.2	14.6	13.9	13.3	12.7	12.1	11.6
94	17.3	16.6	15.9	15.2	14.5	13.9	13.2	12.6	12.0	11.5
95	17.3	16.5	15.8	15.1	14.5	13.8	13.2	12.6	12.0	11.4
96	17.2	16.5	15.8	15.1	14.4	13.8	13.1	12.5	11.9	11.3
97	17.2	16.5	15.8	15.1	14.4	13.7	13.1	12.5	11.9	11.3
98	17.2	16.4	15.7	15.0	14.3	13.7	13.0	12.4	11.8	11.2
99	17.2	16.4	15.7	15.0	14.3	13.6	13.0	12.4	11.8	11.2
100	17.1	16.4	15.7	15.0	14.3	13.6	12.9	12.3	11.7	11.1
101	17.1	16.4	15.6	14.9	14.2	13.6	12.9	12.3	11.7	11.1
102	17.1	16.4	15.6	14.9	14.2	13.5	12.9	12.2	11.6	11.0

Ages	70	71	72	73	74	75	76	77	78	79
103	17.1	16.3	15.6	14.9	14.2	13.5	12.9	12.2	11.6	11.0
104	17.1	16.3	15.6	14.9	14.2	13.5	12.8	12.2	11.6	11.0
105	17.1	16.3	15.6	14.9	14.2	13.5	12.8	12.2	11.5	10.9
106	17.1	16.3	15.6	14.8	14.1	13.5	12.8	12.2	11.5	10.9
107	17.0	16.3	15.6	14.8	14.1	13.4	12.8	12.1	11.5	10.9
108	17.0	16.3	15.5	14.8	14.1	13.4	12.8	12.1	11.5	10.9
109	17.0	16.3	15.5	14.8	14.1	13.4	12.8	12.1	11.5	10.9
110	17.0	16.3	15.5	14.8	14.1	13.4	12.7	12.1	11.5	10.9
111	17.0	16.3	15.5	14.8	14.1	13.4	12.7	12.1	11.5	10.8
112	17.0	16.3	15.5	14.8	14.1	13.4	12.7	12.1	11.5	10.8
113	17.0	16.3	15.5	14.8	14.1	13.4	12.7	12.1	11.4	10.8
114	17.0	16.3	15.5	14.8	14.1	13.4	12.7	12.1	11.4	10.8
115+	17.0	16.3	15.5	14.8	14.1	13.4	12.7	12.1	11.4	10.8

Ages	80	81	82	83	84	85	86	87	88	89
80	13.8	13.4	13.1	12.8	12.6	12.3	12.1	11.9	11.7	11.5
81	13.4	13.1	12.7	12.4	12.2	11.9	11.7	11.4	11.3	11.1
82	13.1	12.7	12.4	12.1	11.8	11.5	11.3	11.0	10.8	10.6
83	12.8	12.4	12.1	11.7	11.4	11.1	10.9	10.6	10.4	10.2
84	12.6	12.2	11.8	11.4	11.1	10.8	10.5	10.3	10.1	9.9
85	12.3	11.9	11.5	11.1	10.8	10.5	10.2	9.9	9.7	9.5
86	12.1	11.7	11.3	10.9	10.5	10.2	9.9	9.6	9.4	9.2

Ages	80	81	82	83	84	85	86	87	88	89
87	11.9	11.4	11.0	10.6	10.3	9.9	9.6	9.4	9.1	8.9
88	11.7	11.3	10.8	10.4	10.1	9.7	9.4	9.1	8.8	8.6
89	11.5	11.1	10.6	10.2	9.9	9.5	9.2	8.9	8.6	8.3
90	11.4	10.9	10.5	10.1	9.7	9.3	9.0	8.6	8.3	8.1
91	11.3	10.8	10.3	9.9	9.5	9.1	8.8	8.4	8.1	7.9
92	11.2	10.7	10.2	9.8	9.3	9.0	8.6	8.3	8.0	7.7
93	11.1	10.6	10.1	9.6	9.2	8.8	8.5	8.1	7.8	7.5
94	11.0	10.5	10.0	9.5	9.1	8.7	8.3	8.0	7.6	7.3
95	10.9	10.4	9.9	9.4	9.0	8.6	8.2	7.8	7.5	7.2
96	10.8	10.3	9.8	9.3	8.9	8.5	8.1	7.7	7.4	7.1
97	10.7	10.2	9.7	9.2	8.8	8.4	8.0	7.6	7.3	6.9
98	10.7	10.1	9.6	9.2	8.7	8.3	7.9	7.5	7.1	6.8
99	10.6	10.1	9.6	9.1	8.6	8.2	7.8	7.4	7.0	6.7
100	10.6	10.0	9.5	9.0	8.5	8.1	7.7	7.3	6.9	6.6
101	10.5	10.0	9.4	9.0	8.5	8.0	7.6	7.2	6.9	6.5
102	10.5	9.9	9.4	8.9	8.4	8.0	7.5	7.1	6.8	6.4
103	10.4	9.9	9.4	8.8	8.4	7.9	7.5	7.1	6.7	6.3
104	10.4	9.8	9.3	8.8	8.3	7.9	7.4	7.0	6.6	6.3
105	10.4	9.8	9.3	8.8	8.3	7.8	7.4	7.0	6.6	6.2
106	10.3	9.8	9.2	8.7	8.2	7.8	7.3	6.9	6.5	6.2
107	10.3	9.8	9.2	8.7	8.2	7.7	7.3	6.9	6.5	6.1

Ages	80	81	82	83	84	85	86	87	88	89
108	10.3	9.7	9.2	8.7	8.2	7.7	7.3	6.8	6.4	6.1
109	10.3	9.7	9.2	8.7	8.2	7.7	7.2	6.8	6.4	6.0
110	10.3	9.7	9.2	8.6	8.1	7.7	7.2	6.8	6.4	6.0
111	10.3	9.7	9.1	8.6	8.1	7.6	7.2	6.8	6.3	6.0
112	10.2	9.7	9.1	8.6	8.1	7.6	7.2	6.7	6.3	5.9
113	10.2	9.7	9.1	8.6	8.1	7.6	7.2	6.7	6.3	5.9
114	10.2	9.7	9.1	8.6	8.1	7.6	7.1	6.7	6.3	5.9
115+	10.2	9.7	9.1	8.6	8.1	7.6	7.1	6.7	6.3	5.9

Ages	90	91	92	93	94	95	96	97	98	99
90	7.8	7.6	7.4	7.2	7.1	6.9	6.8	6.6	6.5	6.4
91	7.6	7.4	7.2	7.0	6.8	6.7	6.5	6.4	6.3	6.1
92	7.4	7.2	7.0	6.8	6.6	6.4	6.3	6.1	6.0	5.9
93	7.2	7.0	6.8	6.6	6.4	6.2	6.1	5.9	5.8	5.6
94	7.1	6.8	6.6	6.4	6.2	6.0	5.9	5.7	5.6	5.4
95	6.9	6.7	6.4	6.2	6.0	5.8	5.7	5.5	5.4	5.2
96	6.8	6.5	6.3	6.1	5.9	5.7	5.5	5.3	5.2	5.0
97	6.6	6.4	6.1	5.9	5.7	5.5	5.3	5.2	5.0	4.9
98	6.5	6.3	6.0	5.8	5.6	5.4	5.2	5.0	4.8	4.7
99	6.4	6.1	5.9	5.6	5.4	5.2	5.0	4.9	4.7	4.5
100	6.3	6.0	5.8	5.5	5.3	5.1	4.9	4.7	4.5	4.4
101	6.2	5.9	5.6	5.4	5.2	5.0	4.8	4.6	4.4	4.2

Ages	90	91	92	93	94	95	96	97	98	99
102	6.1	5.8	5.5	5.3	5.1	4.8	4.6	4.4	4.3	4.1
103	6.0	5.7	5.4	5.2	5.0	4.7	4.5	4.3	4.1	4.0
104	5.9	5.6	5.4	5.1	4.9	4.6	4.4	4.2	4.0	3.8
105	5.9	5.6	5.3	5.0	4.8	4.5	4.3	4.1	3.9	3.7
106	5.8	5.5	5.2	4.9	4.7	4.5	4.2	4.0	3.8	3.6
107	5.8	5.4	5.1	4.9	4.6	4.4	4.2	3.9	3.7	3.5
108	5.7	5.4	5.1	4.8	4.6	4.3	4.1	3.9	3.7	3.5
109	5.7	5.3	5.0	4.8	4.5	4.3	4.0	3.8	3.6	3.4
110	5.6	5.3	5.0	4.7	4.5	4.2	4.0	3.8	3.5	3.3
111	5.6	5.3	5.0	4.7	4.4	4.2	3.9	3.7	3.5	3.3
112	5.6	5.3	4.9	4.7	4.4	4.1	3.9	3.7	3.5	3.2
113	5.6	5.2	4.9	4.6	4.4	4.1	3.9	3.6	3.4	3.2
114	5.6	5.2	4.9	4.6	4.3	4.1	3.9	3.6	3.4	3.2
115+	5.5	5.2	4.9	4.6	4.3	4.1	3.8	3.6	3.4	3.1

Ages	100	101	102	103	104	105	106	107	108	109
100	4.2	4.1	3.9	3.8	3.7	3.5	3.4	3.3	3.3	3.2
101	4.1	3.9	3.7	3.6	3.5	3.4	3.2	3.1	3.1	3.0
102	3.9	3.7	3.6	3.4	3.3	3.2	3.1	3.0	2.9	2.8
103	3.8	3.6	3.4	3.3	3.2	3.0	2.9	2.8	2.7	2.6
104	3.7	3.5	3.3	3.2	3.0	2.9	2.7	2.6	2.5	2.4
105	3.5	3.4	3.2	3.0	2.9	2.7	2.6	2.5	2.4	2.3

Ages	100	101	102	103	104	105	106	107	108	109
106	3.4	3.2	3.1	2.9	2.7	2.6	2.4	2.3	2.2	2.1
107	3.3	3.1	3.0	2.8	2.6	2.5	2.3	2.2	2.1	2.0
108	3.3	3.1	2.9	2.7	2.5	2.4	2.2	2.1	1.9	1.8
109	3.2	3.0	2.8	2.6	2.4	2.3	2.1	2.0	1.8	1.7
110	3.1	2.9	2.7	2.5	2.3	2.2	2.0	1.9	1.7	1.6
111	3.1	2.9	2.7	2.5	2.3	2.1	1.9	1.8	1.6	1.5
112	3.0	2.8	2.6	2.4	2.2	2.0	1.9	1.7	1.5	1.4
113	3.0	2.8	2.6	2.4	2.2	2.0	1.8	1.6	1.5	1.3
114	3.0	2.7	2.5	2.3	2.1	1.9	1.8	1.6	1.4	1.3
115+	2.9	2.7	2.5	2.3	2.1	1.9	1.7	1.5	1.4	1.2

Ages	110	111	112	113	114	115+
110	1.5	1.4	1.3	1.2	1.1	1.1
111	1.4	1.2	1.1	1.1	1.0	1.0
112	1.3	1.1	1.0	1.0	1.0	1.0
113	1.2	1.1	1.0	1.0	1.0	1.0
114	1.1	1.0	1.0	1.0	1.0	1.0
115+	1.1	1.0	1.0	1.0	1.0	1.0

Source: Treasury Regulations.

Bibliography

Craig, Michael. *The 5 Minute Investor.* Franklin Lakes, N.J.: Career Press, 2002.

Daryanani, Gobind. *Roth IRA Book.* Bernardsville, N.J.: Digiqual, Inc.: 1998.

DeLapa, Gina. *401(k) Success Stories.* Kalamazoo, Mich.: Financial Literacy Center, 2000.

Edmunds, Gillette. *Comfort Zone Investing.* Franklin Lakes, N.J.: Career Press, 2002.

EMJAY Corporation. *401(k) Answer Book.* New York: Aspen Publishers, 2002.

Fox, Loren. *Enron: The Rise and Fall.* Hoboken, N.J.: John Wiley & Sons, 2003.

Fusaro, Peter C. and Ross M. Miller. *What Went Wrong at Enron.* Hoboken, N.J.: John Wiley & Sons, 2002.

Gokhale, Jagadeesh, Laurence J. Kotlikoff, and Todd Neumann. "Does Participating in a 401(k) Raise Your Lifetime Taxes?" Research paper sponsored by Boston University, the Smith-Richardson Foundation, and the National Institute of Aging. May 2001.

Kindleberger, Charles P. *Manias, Panics, and Crashes.* New York: John Wiley & Sons, 2000.

Levitt, Arthur with Paula Dwyer. *Take on the Street*. New York: Pantheon Books, 2002.

Malkiel, Burton G. *A Random Walk Down Wall Street*. New York: W.W. Norton & Company, 1999.

Morris, Virginia B. and Kenneth M. Morris. *Essential Guide to Your 401(k) Plan*. New York: Lightbulb Press, 2001.

O'Glove, Thornton L. *Quality of Earnings*. New York: The Free Press, 1987.

Purcell, Patrick J. "Retirement Savings and Household Wealth in 2000: Analysis of Census Bureau Data." Congressional Research Service Report for Congress. Updated December 12, 2002.

Rye, David E. *1,001 Ways to Save, Grow, and Invest Your Money*. Franklin Lakes, N.J.: Career Press, 1999.

Stanley, Thomas J. *The Millionaire Mind*. Kansas City, Mo.: Andrews McMeel Publishing, 2002.

Weinstein, Grace W. *J.K. Lasser's Winning with Your 401(k)*. New York: John Wiley & Sons, 2001.

Weiss, Martin D. *The Ultimate Safe Money Guide*. New York: John Wiley & Sons, 2002.

Wolff, Edward N. *Retirement Insecurity: The Income Shortfalls Awaiting the Soon-to-Retire*. Washington, D.C.: Economic Policy Institute, 2002.

Woodhouse, Violet and Dale Fethering. *Divorce & Money*. Berkeley, Calif.: Nolo, 2000.

Glossary

Active management. An investment portfolio management strategy that seeks to exceed the rate of return of a selected market index.

Age 50 catch-up contributions. Additional 401(k) or IRA contributions that individuals who are age 50 or older may make.

Alternate payee. An individual other than the 401(k) account owner (such as a spouse, former spouse, or child) who, under a qualified domestic relations order, has a right to receive all or some of the money in a 401(k) account.

Annuity. A contract that provides income at regular intervals. (See joint and survivor annuity and qualified joint and survivor annuity.)

Asset allocation. The process of deciding how investment dollars will be divided among available investment alternatives.

Audit. A professional examination and verification of a company's financial statements for the purpose of rendering an independent opinion as to their conformity with generally accepted accounting principles.

Auditor. A skilled professional who audits a company's financial statements.

Bear market. A prolonged decline in the prices of stocks, bonds, or commodities.

Behavioral finance. A school of thought that seeks to explain stock price movements as reflecting changing investor perceptions of what other investors will be willing to pay for the stock in the future.

Beneficiary. An individual who or entity that is designated to receive property in the event of the property owner's death.

Bond. A type of debt instrument that is issued by corporations, governments, and government agencies. The issuer makes regular interest payments and promises to pay back the face value of the bond at a certain time (called the maturity date).

Bond fund. A mutual fund that invests mostly in bonds.

Bull market. A prolonged increase in the prices of stocks, bonds, or commodities.

Capital gain. The positive difference between the selling price of an asset and its cost or other basis.

Compensation. The amount of a 401(k) participant's pay that is considered for the purposes of certain employee benefits.

Deemed IRA. An optional 401(k) plan feature that allows plan sponsors to deduct traditional IRA and Roth IRA contributions directly from employees' pay.

Defined benefit plan. A traditional retirement plan in which the employer provides retirees with a regular retirement income for life.

Defined contribution plan. An employer-sponsored plan in which contributions are made to individual employee accounts. The benefit to the employee consists solely of investments and investment returns that have accumulated in these individual accounts.

Deflation. Overall decline in the prices of goods and services. The opposite of inflation.

Department of Labor (DOL). The federal department that deals with issues related to American workers, including pension and other employee benefits. Through its branch agency, the Employee Benefits Security Administration, the DOL enforces workers' rights under ERISA.

Direct rollover. The transfer of an eligible rollover distribution directly to the trustee of another retirement savings plan.

Disclosure. The access to certain documents that plan sponsors must provide to plan participants, including summary plan descriptions, summary of material modifications, and summary annual reports.

Distribution. Any payout from a retirement plan. (See annuity and lump-sum distribution.)

Diversification. A strategy for investing in different types of investments to reduce the risk of investing in a single investment.

Early withdrawal penalty. The 10-percent penalty for withdrawing money from a 401(k) plan before retirement. This penalty is in addition to regular federal tax and state tax, if applicable.

Economic Growth and Tax Relief Reconciliation Act of 2001 (EGTRRA). A 2001 tax law that contained many changes to the retirement plan rules.

Eligibility. The conditions that must be met to participate in a 401(k) plan, such as age or years of service.

Eligible employee. An employee who may participate in a 401(k) plan.

Eligible rollover distribution. A distribution from a 401(k) account, except for certain periodic distributions, minimum distributions, and the portion of a distribution that represents a return of employee contributions.

Employee Benefits Security Administration (EBSA). A federal agency established by ERISA for the insurance of traditional pension plans. The PBGC pays pension benefits to retirees if a traditional pension plan can't cover all required benefits to retirees.

Employee Retirement Income Security Act of 1974 (ERISA). A federal law that includes both tax rules, which pertain to requirements for tax benefits, and Department of Labor provisions, which pertain to the rights of participants and beneficiaries and the obligations of plan fiduciaries. The law applies to 401(k) plan sponsors as to plan design and administration.

Employer stock. Shares of stock that are issued by a corporation that sponsors a 401(k) plan.

Expected earnings. The forecast of a company's future earnings.

Federal Reserve Bank (the Fed). The system that was established by the Federal Reserve Act of 1913 to regulate the U.S. monetary and banking system.

Fiduciary. An individual with the authority to make decisions about a 401(k) plan and its administration. ERISA requires fiduciaries to make decisions according to the best interests of 401(k) account owners.

Filing status. The U.S. taxpayer category that an individual chooses when filing an income tax return. The choices are single, married filing joint, married filing separately, and head of household.

Form ADV. The uniform application for investment adviser registration that is used to register with the Securities and Exchange Commission or with a state securities authority.

Form 1099-R. An IRS form that is sent to an individual who receives a 401(k) plan distribution. The form is also filed with the IRS.

Form 5329. An IRS form for reporting additional taxes (the 10-percent penalty) on qualified plans, IRAs, and other tax-favored accounts.

Form 5500. An IRS form that all 401(k) plans must prepare and file with the IRS every year.

Fundamental analysis. The analysis of whether a particular stock is undervalued or overvalued at the current market price, based on an appraisal of the company's future prospects.

Guaranteed investment contract (GIC). A contract with an insurance company in which the insurance company is obligated to repay the principal at a designated future date and to pay interest at a specified rate over the duration of the contract.

Hardship distribution. A 401(k) plan participant's withdrawal of his or her plan contributions before retirement, if the employer permits. Distribution eligibility may be based on a financial hardship. These distributions are taxable as premature distributions and are subject to a 10-percent penalty if the recipient is under age 59½.

Index. A benchmark indicator that shows the value of a representative group of securities. Examples include the Dow Jones Industrial Average and the Standard & Poor's 500.

Index fund. A mutual fund that seeks to match the performance of a particular stock market index or bond market index.

Individual retirement account (IRA). A personal investment vehicle that an eligible individual may use to make annual tax-deductible contributions or to roll over eligible distributions from a 401(k) plan.

These accounts must meet tax code requirements, but they are not part of any employer-sponsored plan.

Internal Revenue Service (IRS). The branch of the U.S. Treasury Department that administers certain requirements of qualified plans and other retirement investment vehicles. The IRS also works with the DOL and the EBSA to develop Form 5500 and now monitors the data that employers submit annually.

Investment alternative. An investment choice in a 401(k) plan, such as employer stock, a money market fund, or an index fund.

Joint and survivor annuity. An annuity that is paid for the life of a particular individual, with payments that continue for the life of his or her spouse.

Junk bonds. Bonds that carry an above-average credit risk but promise an above-average rate of return.

Levy. The act of collecting a tax.

Liquid. Easily convertible to cash.

Liquidate. To convert into cash.

Lump-sum distribution. The distribution of a 401(k) owner's entire account balance when he or she leaves the employer.

Marginal tax rate. The percentage of tax that is imposed on an additional dollar of income.

Matching contribution. A contribution that an employer makes to a 401(k) account, based on the contributions that the employee made.

Material modification. A change in the terms of a 401(k) plan that may affect participants.

Money market account. A bank account that pays interest at market rates.

Money market fund. A mutual fund that seeks to generate income for investors using short-term investments.

Monte Carlo simulation. A sophisticated retirement planning tool that uses randomness to help predict adequate retirement savings.

Mortality table. An organized chart of life expectancies based on age and other relevant factors.

Mutual fund. An investment fund with a diversified range of investments, thus reducing the risk to each investor participating in the fund.

Net asset value. The price that members of the public may pay to buy a share in a mutual fund.

No-load fund. A mutual fund that does not charge a sales commission.

Ordinary income. Income from an individual's ordinary activities, as distinguished from capital gains from the sale of assets.

Participant. An employee or former employee who owns an account in a 401(k) plan.

Participant loan. A loan from a 401(k) plan to a participant.

Pension and Welfare Benefits Administration (PWBA). The branch of the Department of Labor that protects the pensions, health plans, and other employee benefits of American workers. The PWBA enforces ERISA's rules for reporting, disclosure, vesting, participation, funding, and fiduciary conduct.

Pension fund. Money set aside by an employer to pay the traditional pension benefits of retired workers.

Plan administrator. The individual, group, or company that is responsible for day-to-day operations of a 401(k) plan. Generally speaking, the plan sponsor is the plan administrator.

Plan loan. A loan from a participant's 401(k) account, which cannot exceed 50 percent of the balance or $50,000, whichever is less.

Plan participant. An individual who has an account in a 401(k) plan.

Plan sponsor. The employer that established and is maintaining the 401(k) plan.

Portfolio. The combined holding of many securities and other investments to reduce the risk of loss through diversification.

Pre-tax contribution. Money that is subtracted from your pay and put into tax-advantaged retirement savings before income taxes are imposed on your pay.

Price/earnings (P/E) ratio. The ratio of a stock's current price to its earnings per share. The P/E ratio of a mutual fund or a stock market index is the weighted average of the P/E ratios of the stocks that it holds.

Principal. The original amount invested, exclusive of earnings.

Profit sharing plan. An employer-sponsored plan funded only by employer contributions. Employer contributions may be determined by a fixed formula related to the employer's profits or may be at the discretion of the company's board of directors.

Prospectus. A document that is issued by a mutual fund or other investment opportunity to describe the history, investment objectives, financial statements, background of managers, and other relevant information.

Public company. A corporation that issued shares of stock to members of the general public.

Qualified Domestic Relations Order (QDRO). A court order that creates or recognizes an alternate payee's (such as former spouse, or child) right to receive all or a portion of a participant's 401(k) account balance.

Qualified joint and survivor annuity (QJSA). An annuity with payments that continue to the surviving spouse after the 401(k) owner's death, equal to at least 50 percent of the participant's benefit.

Qualified plan. Any plan, including a 401(k) plan, a 403(b) plan, or a 457 plan, among others, that qualifies for favorable tax treatment by meeting the requirements of the federal tax code and by following certain regulations.

Rate of return. The dividend yield plus capital appreciation.

Rebalance. To shift money from one investment alternative to another according to a predetermined allocation scheme or formula.

Registered investment advisor (RIA). An investment advisor who is registered either with the SEC or with the state in which the advisor maintains his or her principal office and business.

Reported earnings. A public company's release of its earnings data to the general public, usually in audited financial statements.

Required minimum distribution (RMD). The amount that must be withdrawn each year from a 401(k) plan once the account owner reaches age 70½ or retires, if later.

Restated earnings. Corrected information about a corporation's earnings that were previously misstated.

Risk tolerance. An individual's personal willingness or ability to accept declining values of his or her investments.

Rollover. The action of moving 401(k) plan funds from one qualified plan to another or to an IRA within 60 days of distributions, which retains the tax deferral.

Roth IRA. A type of IRA that is funded with after-tax dollars. Qualifying distributions from a Roth IRA are tax-free.

Rule 12b-1 fee. An ongoing fee that is paid out of mutual fund assets.

Rule 12b-1 fees may be used to pay commissions to brokers and other salespersons, to pay for advertising and other costs of promoting the fund to investors, and to pay various service providers to a 401(k) plan according to a bundled services arrangement.

Securities and Exchange Commission (SEC). A federal agency that administers laws that are designed to protect investors against malpractice in the securities markets.

Security. An instrument that represents part ownership of a corporation (a stock) or a creditor relationship with a corporation or governmental entity (a bond).

Service provider. An outside firm that provides any type of service to the 401(k) plan, including managing assets, record-keeping, providing plan education, and administering the plan.

Stable value investment. A relatively low-risk investment, such as a money market fund or a guaranteed investment contract.

Standard & Poor's 500 (S&P 500). A broad-based measurement of changes in the stock market, based on the performance of 500 widely held common stocks.

Stock. A security that represents part ownership, or equity, in a corporation.

Stock fund. A mutual fund that invests in stocks.

Stockholders' equity. An amount equal to a corporation's assets minus its liabilities (debt).

Stock market. The organized trading of stocks through the various stock exchanges and the over-the-counter market.

Substantially equal periodic payments. A series of distributions from a 401(k) account that are made over the life of the account owner or the joint lives of the account owner and his or her spouse.

Summary plan description (SPD). A document that describes in plain English the features of a particular 401(k) plan. The primary purpose of the SPD is to disclose the features of the plan to current and potential plan participants. ERISA requires that the SPD contain certain information, including participant rights under ERISA, claims procedures, and funding arrangements.

Traditional IRA. A type of IRA that is generally funded with pre-tax contributions or rollovers from a qualified plan. Distributions are generally taxable.

Traditional pension. Regular income payments to a former employee who met certain age and years of work service requirements.

Treasury securities. Negotiable debt obligations of the U.S. government, which are issued at various maturities.

Trust. A legal entity that is recognized under state law and that holds and administers assets for the beneficiaries of or participants in the entity.

Trustee. The individual, bank, or trust company that has fiduciary responsibility for holding trust assets.

Vesting. A participant's right to employer contributions that have accrued in his or her individual 401(k) account.

Vesting schedule. The structure for determining a participant's right to employer contributions that have accrued in his or her individual 401(k) account. In a 401(k) plan with immediate vesting, employee contributions are fully vested as soon as they are deposited in a participant's account.

Volatility. The characteristic of a security, commodity, or market to rise and fall sharply in price within a short time period.

Index

J

Joint and survivor annuity, definition of, 172

Junk bonds, definition of, 172

L

Levy, definition of, 172

Lifetime Savings Accounts, 12

Liquid, definition of, 172

Liquidate, definition of, 172

Loads, 72

Loans, 92-93

Losing money, 16

Lump-sum distribution, definition of, 172

M

Management fees, 25, 72

Marginal tax rate, definition of, 172

Market booms, 18

Market crashes, 18

Market volatility, protecting from, 15-26

Matching contribution, 45 definition of, 172

Material modification, definition of, 172

Mean, definition of, 39

Median, definition of, 39

Misconduct, employer, 53-67

Money market account, definition of, 172

Money market fund, definition of, 172

Money, losing, 16 taking out wisely, 81-98

Monte Carlo simulation, 40-41 definition of, 173

Mortality table, definition of, 173

Mutual funds, 73-75 definition of, 173

N

Net asset value, definition of, 173

No-load fund, definition of, 173

O

Ordinary income, definition of, 173

P

Participant, definition of, 173

Participant loan, definition of, 173

Paying financial advisors, 116

Penalty, 10-percent, 85

Pension and Welfare Benefits Administration, definition of, 173

About
the Author

ELIZABETH OPALKA IS A CPA LICENSED in Maryland and an attorney admitted to practice law in New York, Connecticut, and Florida. Ms. Opalka majored in finance at Indiana University, earned her master's degree in taxation from the State University of New York at Albany, and received her law degree from Albany Law School. Today, she lives and works in the Albany, New York, area.

For a one-year subscription to Elizabeth Opalka's Retirement Newsletter, published monthly, please send a check for $14 to:

Elizabeth Opalka's Retirement Newsletter
2431 Rosendale Road
Niskayuna, NY 12309